HOW TO WRITE
FILLERS
AND
SHORT FEATURES
THAT SELL
* * * * * *

Louise Boggess

HOW TO WRITE FILLERS AND SHORT FEATURES THAT SELL

* * * * * * *

Second Edition

HARPER & ROW, PUBLISHERS, New York
Cambridge, Philadelphia, San Francisco,
London, Mexico City, São Paulo, Sydney

1817

The author makes grateful acknowledgment to the publishers who granted permission to reprint material used in this book. A complete listing of their publications can be found in the Markets section beginning on page 164.

Designed by Ruth Bornschlegel

Library of Congress Cataloging in Publication Data
Boggess, Louise.
How to write fillers and short features that sell.
Includes index.
1. Authorship. I. Title.
PN147.B616 1981   808'.02   80-8682
ISBN 0-06-010492-9

81 82 83 84 85 10 9 8 7 6 5 4 3 2 1

To my children, Pat and Bill,
who have done so much to complete the pages of my life

Contents

CONTENTS

Preface

In the past when the copy did not completely fill the printed page, a frugal printer added a helpful household hint, a pithy bit of advice, or an amusing anecdote. Later someone referred to these "copy extenders" as *fillers*—or so the story goes. Originally most editors defined fillers as short pieces of less than three hundred words. As the demand for fillers increased, editors extended the word limit and appealed to readers for contributions.

Today reader contributions have so greatly popularized fillers that a number of magazines group them under special titles, such as "Life in These United States" in *Reader's Digest*, while still continuing the end-of-the-page ones. Some editors request contributions to regular by-lined columns in the form of newsbreaks or information on new products.

In like manner the introduction of mini-articles—informative, how-to-do-it, self-help, to name a few—has led to special sections, such as "Right Now" in *McCall's*, "The Better Way" in *Good Housekeeping*, and "Almanac" in *Sports Afield*. The confession magazines often place these mini-features in single columns alongside of a page or set them apart in a box.

In addition to these mini-features, a number of magazines urge readers to contribute personal-problem experiences or opinions on any subject in articles varying in length from three hundred to two thousand words. Contributions from readers have become so important that the tables of contents in magazines often list them under "departments" or "regular features."

This expanding market offers anyone an opportunity to write and sell fillers and short features. To help you sell your pieces, this book not only shows you where to look for ideas but also explains and illustrates the few simple writing techniques you need to learn. In order to make learning these techniques easier, the book analyzes specific published examples from a variety of magazines and groups them in categories. The market list that begins on page 164 supplies the names and addresses of the magazines that use fillers as well as a brief description of the kind of material each one accepts.

Once you make your first sale, you will want to try again. To profit most from this book, use it as a reference source. When you find an idea, check for the correct techniques and probable markets before you actually write the piece. Then read the magazine. By using this approach you can sell to any market.

The information discussed in this book comes from twenty years of analyzing the filler market and selling short features, numerous discussions in person and by mail with editors, and fifteen years of teaching others how to write fillers and short features. Students in my professional writing classes helped me test my analyses by selling fillers to designated markets. They proved to my satisfaction that knowing how to write for a particular market pays dividends. Letters from those who bought the previous edition, *Writing Fillers That Sell,* also stated they made repeated sales.

My sincere appreciation goes to the editors, far too many to name individually, who assisted me by sending tear sheets of their fillers and features and granted me permission to reprint the examples that appear in this book. I am deeply indebted to the students who helped me test this market. Without the encouragement and assistance of my husband as my favorite critic, I could not have updated this book.

Louise Boggess

San Mateo, California

By the time a writer discovers he has no talent
for literature, he is too successful to give it up.
—*Robert Benchley*

1*
Get Set

At a luncheon the woman sitting beside me pointed to her overweight friend at the end of the table and remarked, "She bought a reducing machine last week for a ridiculous price."

The comment kept cropping up in my mind all during the luncheon as a possible filler, but it needed revising for a laugh. Before I arrived home several hours later I found the answer and quickly wrote in my notebook: "Substitute 'figure' for 'price' so statement reads, 'She bought a reducing machine last week for a ridiculous figure.'" This slight change made the incident a salable filler; so learn right now that you must occasionally do a little literary doctoring to make the actual happening amusing.

Fillers and short features offer anyone an exceptional opportunity to write and sell. You can write and sell because the editor buys the material regardless of who wrote it—a known or unknown writer. To a beginning writer, the sale of a recipe or mini-experience, no matter how small the pay, gives encouragement to keep trying. On the other hand, the established writer may find fillers and short pieces while doing research for fiction or nonfiction. These spin-offs can easily cover the cost of research. Finally, many people who have no thought of writing professionally may want to share an experience, but hesitate because they do not know simple writing techniques. Knowing these simple techniques provides the young mother, the senior citizen, the invalid, and many others with the necessary confidence to submit a filler or short feature to any editor.

Fortunately, you can easily learn the necessary techniques in a few hours of writing. You already know most of them but have never found the occasion to use them. Furthermore, writing these short items requires very little actual time. In fact, you simply work on the margins of time by jotting down ideas while you wait in the dentist's office, eat your lunch, or commute to work. Anyone can find ten minutes here or fifteen there to work on a filler.

These jottings can earn you from one hundred to three hundred dollars a month. In addition, think of the satisfaction you derive from sharing some special knowledge, a bit of laughter, an interesting personality, or a dramatic experience with literally thousands of readers. A mother of eight children confided in a letter that selling an anecdote won her the respect of both her family and her friends.

Rarely do fillers and short features come to you ready to submit; you must search for them. With a little concentrated looking, you can discover ideas all around you.

RECOGNIZING IDEAS

Think of these short items as brief playbacks from life. To find these playbacks become aware of what people do, say, or think. The more you socialize with people, the more ideas you will collect. So begin your search by observing the world around you.

1. **Observe Everything** When you travel, look for humorous signs on marquees, in front of stores, in store display windows, on panel trucks, or on billboards. Small towns or wayside cafés offer very fertile ground for this type of filler. A sign on the highway advertised: "You Came You Saw Utah." One cafe placed on the menu a "Hangover Breakfast: 2 poached eggs, large tomato juice, 2 aspirins, coffee, and our sympathy."

This sign appeared on a cement-mixer truck: "We find a need and fill it." A carpet store advertised: "Our Prices Will Floor You." A sign in a pawn shop window urged: "See us at your earliest inconvenience." A church billboard promised: "Life's Fragile—handle with prayer."

A sign in an unexpected place led to the sale of an anecdote. During a heavy California rain, the drainage systems overflowed and water reached the doorways of many homes in a housing tract.

One owner promptly put up this homemade sign: "For Sale Cheap This Lakeside Property."

Actions of people, like their words, make good fillers. Never wait aimlessly in an airport or any place crowded with people, but rather study the actions and reactions of those around you. Such observation produced an excellent hint for traveling with youngsters. A young mother between planes at the airport handed her youngster a plastic sack filled with blocks. He dumped the blocks made of colored sponges on the floor without a sound. This suggested a helpful hint the observer was able to sell.

Emotional actions and reactions of people suggest good anecdotes. In an adult-education class for the foreign-born, the teacher asked each person to either sing or recite his national anthem as a means of getting acquainted. When the turn of a Hungarian refugee came, he refused to sing the song of his country but proudly burst into "God Bless America."

Your power of observation can lead you to shortcuts and tips. A few hours with a gourmet cook, a person who keeps an orderly home, or a do-it-yourself handyman can supply you with a large number of ideas. One mother found that tying a knot in two separate corners of a top sheet on a boy's bed made a contour that kept the cover tucked. A spray to remove spots from washable clothes also works well on synthetic carpets.

No editor requires that you discover the shortcut yourself. Go beyond observing action and learn to listen to what people say.

2. Listen to People No one needs a license to listen, but you can profit from what you hear. When a proud parent wants to tell you about the bright sayings of a child, listen. If a friend relates a funny conversation overheard at a cocktail party, get every detail; ask questions if necessary. By adding a few words here and there or shifting them for a more amusing effect, you may sell an anecdote or joke.

Tune in on the conversations of others while you wait in a crowd or commute to work. Two secretaries discussed another person while waiting in a lunch line. "She uses all the brains she has," one said.

The other quipped, "And all she can borrow." A woman in a theater line explained to her friend how she mended the finger of her glove by using a lipstick case as a darning egg.

Family or college reunions make good listening posts. Everyone replays memories of the "good old days," so you hear a wealth of sayings, puns, or humorous incidents. You may want to take along a tape recorder to gather information and later play it at your leisure in searching for ideas. One person remarked, "Their relationship was purely platonic—play for her and tonic for him."

Many lecturers often open a speech or pace remarks with humor. Listen with notebook in hand to any lecturer, luncheon speaker, disc jockey, or stand-up comedian. Do some gleaning from television, radio, or comedy records. One speaker stated, "I learned some time ago that the best ingredient of a good speech was shortening."

When you start to listen, you don't want to stop and write. But you need not depend entirely on observing actions in crowds or listening to people; you can find ideas while you read.

3. Read Everything When you read, keep pen and pad available, for you don't always recall that odd bit of information or that cleverly turned phrase. In biographies look for odd or intimate glimpses of famous people and in all types of writing for an author's salable words. In a short story a character may complain to another, "He's a fanatic because he pays too much attention to his own ideas and too little to mine." Poetry provides excellent imagery and figures of speech which can sell as fillers. Study all of these sources for eye-catching phrases, clever puns, or humorous statements.

When you submit a long quotation from copyrighted material, you will need permission from the publisher and possibly the author. A letter to the publisher will provide the necessary information for a release to reprint. Some magazines pay the originator as well as the one who submits the filler.

Books of quotations stimulate your mind to think in epigrams and quips. In one such book I found this quotation from O. Henry: "A straw vote only shows which way hot air blows." These books may focus on humorous, well-known, or popular quotations. The copyright covers the arrangement of the book, but the actual words of famous people belong to anyone to quote. Form the habit of buying paperbacks of quotations, which cost little compared to what you can earn selling epigrams and quips.

Get in the habit of reading fillers regularly in the magazines. One filler may free your subconscious to recall a similar incident. You have heard the old expression, "That's not the way I heard it." Often in reading a filler you see the possibility of an entirely different version for another market. Take "Old columnists never die—they just go out of print." A similar one could state, "Old bookkeepers never die—they just lose their balance." Try doing some spin-offs yourself on this one.

Don't restrict your reading to magazines, but consider newspapers, especially the local columnist. Here you will find newsbreaks, oddities, or inspirational experiences. Envelope stuffers that come with your utility bills may suggest a new medical fact. One announced, for instance, a testing device, developed by Dr. Philip Peltzman of the University of California (San Francisco) Medical Center, that can read infant brain-wave responses to sound fed through earphones and detect deafness as early as one day after birth.

Newsletters and in-service publications of organizations often contain filler material. From one newsletter came this unusual fact: "The world's only international streetcar line runs between El Paso, Texas, and Cuidad Juarez, Chihuahua, Mexico."

Read annual reports of corporations for historical facts, new scientific research, or new products. All of these could make good column material. Don't toss sales-and-promotion letters, envelope stuffers, or advertisements into the waste basket until you have scanned them for fillers.

Study your newspaper for funny typographical errors, like this one printed in *Reader's Digest* from a Kentucky newspaper's society page regarding a New Year's Eve party: "The large room was vividly decorated with red noses." ° Headlines may appear funny, too, as in this one published in the same issue of *Reader's Digest* from the Brazil *Herald*: "Birth Control Bears Fruit."

° Copyright © 1966 by The Reader's Digest Association, Inc. Reprinted by permission.

Regular news stories relate antics of animals, odd coincidences, and happenings in the lives of well-known people. Clip the item giving the date and source for a newsbreak. You will need permission, however, to submit copyrighted columns or releases by news syndicates, such as Associated Press or United Press International.

So make any reading you do pay dividends in money as well as shared pleasure.

4. Search Your Experiences Your own experiences will supply many fillers and short features. A woman can train herself to look for ideas as she cleans house, sews, or cooks. If she thinks up ways to entertain children or works out an agreeable solution to a family problem with her husband, she may very likely have material for a sale. Always make notes immediately on the funny sayings of children before you forget them.

A business person looks around the office for shortcuts to better business exactly as a homeowner searches the workshop for better ways of handling home tasks. He or she may also find material from friends for profiles of interesting people or mini-articles.

Everyone has a personal experience to share. Editors look for first-person experiences with problems similar to those of the reader to build circulation for the magazine.

When you become more experienced in searching for material, you will develop a built-in antenna that alerts you immediately to an idea. To get the most from your material, you need efficient organization.

FILING SYSTEM

No two people collect and file ideas exactly alike, but most begin with a basic system and personalize it to individual needs. Much depends on the amount of material you collect and the time you can devote to writing. Filing really begins with the notebook and pen you always carry with you.

1. Notebook and Pen You need only a pen and a notebook to do original or secondary research. *Original* refers to unpublished material while *secondary* means items from published sources. A pen works much better than a lead pencil, which can smear almost beyond legibility. Keep your supplies handy at all times.

In selecting a notebook, choose one with a hard back so as to give you support for writing. I prefer the hard-back memo booklet, 3¼ by 6½ inches, which you can refill and which has a pen hooked into the back. Many commercial companies give these booklets to customers, but you can also purchase them at any stationery counter or store for a nominal fee. The size of a notebook will vary with the individual, but keep it small enough to carry in the pocket of a man's coat or in a woman's purse. Perforated sheets remove easily for later filing.

Since you cannot trust your memory, make your notes complete enough to let you recall the entire situation, especially any clever play on words. Too many times, in a rush, I have recorded only key words. A week later when I typed my notes on cards, I could not remember all the facts by reading my brief notations. Periodically, type this material from notebook to cards for a permanent file.

2. Permanent File Schedule a regular time—if at all possible—to transfer your material from the notebook to your permanent filing system. You not only find ideas easier to classify the sooner you record them, but such a system makes selling easier.

In setting up a permanent file, choose the equipment most convenient for you and for the space you have available. Such equipment must expand easily to hold new material, take care of submitted items, and maintain a record of sold pieces.

I personally prefer a long file box that holds five- by eight-inch cards. The cards handle easily, provide enough space to write the filler completely, and leave space on the back to keep a record of individual submittals by date mailed, date returned, and any pertinent comment.

Other writers favor a combination system of file box and loose-leaf notebook. The file box contains the ideas and the record of submittals, but the notebook holds the carbon copy of the filler or short feature.

Regardless of the filing system you choose, you want to compare your version with the printed one and write in any changes. Summarize these changes on a card or a page of the notebook under "Hints on Techniques" and keep it handy for instant referral. From time to time you will add other specialized techniques or market requirements to this section.

In any filing system, group the ideas in categories: anecdotes, arts and crafts, clippings, column material, daffy definitions, epigrams, figures of speech, gags, games, jokes, newsbreaks, oddities, personal experiences, press errors, profiles, puzzles, quips, recipes, riddles, signs, tips and shortcuts, verse, etc. Most likely you will specialize in only one or two categories, such as anecdotes or newsbreaks; but do remain alert for any of the others.

As you collect ideas, you will discover shortcuts for filing. I put the original source that inspired the item with the submitted version. After several return trips from editors, I again read the incident that suggested the idea to get a new approach that will make it salable. As you work at writing and selling these short pieces, you will find new ways to individualize your file for more efficient service.

In the past, when a magazine bought a short item, it acquired all rights. Today most magazines buy only one-time rights, and the other rights return to you after publication. So never throw away material you have sold, as you may find a way to recycle it.

Now that you know where to look for ideas and how to file them efficiently, you need to learn the necessary writing techniques.

2*
Professional
Writing Techniques

A funny thing happened to you, and you recount the incident to a group of friends and acquaintances. They roar with laughter; yet one editor after another does not buy it. On paper it didn't read amusing. Why? You didn't realize that when you told this story, you used voice tone, facial expressions, and hand motions to project the action. If you could have mailed yourself with the written piece, the editor would have laughed and bought it.

Your written version lacked the writing techniques which project a story to the reader with its humorous impact. While you can easily learn these techniques, you may not recognize these magic ingredients yourself until someone points them out to you. Projection techniques can make the difference between rejection and acceptance. One of the magic devices consists of viewpoint.

VIEWPOINT

"Viewpoint" refers to the focus from which you project the filler or short feature. The item may state the facts objectively or relate them subjectively and personalize them. Whether you use objective or subjective viewpoint depends on the material and the market.

1. Objective Viewpoint Objective viewpoint reports only the facts, without emotion or a personal pronoun. Choose objective viewpoint when you make a statement that will stand alone, on the facts, without the emotional overlay of a person identified by a pronoun as the source. Many quips, epigrams, and quotations fall into this category. Take this example: "Three square meals a day can make a person round." Knowing who made this statement does not add to the impact of the humor.

Even though you may give the name of the person making the statement, you still use objective viewpoint as long as you do not enter the mind of the speaker to give his emotional feelings, as in these examples.

> George Canning stated, "Nothing is so fallacious as facts, except figures."
>
> Franklin P. Adams said, "Dunking is bad taste but tastes good."

Crediting these statements to individuals does not change the objective tone or the humor.

Select objective viewpoint when you report odd facts from the past or present.

> Franciscan padres who established California's missions kept a record of earthquakes. In 1805, an earthquake ruined the roof of Mission San Gabriel. Forty worshipers lost their lives during a quake at San Juan Capistrano on December 8, 1912. Santa Clara Mission had an earthquake in 1812, and again in 1818. A quake destroyed the Santa Barbara Mission Church on June 29, 1925.

Occasionally, you may write a short household or shop tip in objective viewpoint so as to focus on the information. This example relies on objective viewpoint: "Toothpaste will remove a new white ring from dark wood furniture."

Some anecdotes come through with sufficient humor in objective viewpoint, like this one from *Orben's Comedy Fillers.*°

> Overheard in an elevator:
>
> "I had some good news today. I got a thirty-year, 10 percent loan."
>
> "You bought a house?"
>
> "No, a Christmas tree."

° Copyright © 1979 by Robert Orben. Reprinted by permission.

Newsbreaks and new products frequently appear in objective viewpoint, as in this illustration from *The Star,* headlined "Big Apple's Fruitful Foreigners."

> The economy of New York City is now dependent on resident foreign companies, a New York University study shows. It says they employ 8.4 percent of all workers. And if the expansion plans of foreign companies go ahead, total employment would reach 15 percent by 1985.

At times signs may make an objective statement with no need for a personal pronoun. A car body shop put this sign on the billboard: "Metal Menders for Tender Fenders."

At first you want to write everything in objective viewpoint because you learned this form in English composition. But don't make a hasty decision until you see how much subjective viewpoint can improve the projection of certain types of fillers or short features.

2. Subjective Viewpoint In subjective viewpoint you share your emotional reactions with the reader. This viewpoint offers the writer a wide variety of emotional choices.

When you center the action of the filler around the reactions of one person and identify the writer with a pronoun, you employ *single-major-character viewpoint.* This beginning excerpt of an anecdote from "Life in These United States," from *Reader's Digest,* illustrates this viewpoint with the first-person pronoun. †

> Because I had a particularly trying day, I complained bitterly to my husband about the thankless job of being a housewife. I raved on for a while, then decided to answer some mail and pound out my irritability on the typewriter.

Here the author shares her emotional thinking with the reader in first-person major-character viewpoint.

You may write the item from third-person major character view-

†Copyright © 1966 by The Reader's Digest Association, Inc. Reprinted by permission.

point, as in this example from "Personal Glimpses" in *Reader's Digest*.[‡] I use only the opening paragraph here—not the entire piece.

> Danny Kaye always hoped he might be a doctor. Today he follows medicine the way some people follow their favorite sport.

We step into the mind of the major character, Danny Kaye, but use the third-person pronoun *he* for identification.

Sometimes a single minor character relates what another person does, as in this paragraph from an anecdote in "Life in These United States," *Reader's Digest*.[§]

> Having learned most of his driving in a horse-drawn buggy, my father was prone to absent-mindedness behind the wheel of his pickup truck.

The writer, the minor character, tells about his father, the major character.

In some fillers and short features the writer never identifies the narrator with a personal pronoun, but you feel someone relates the facts emotionally. This illustration from *Fate* shows the implied narrator.

> Grendel, the "monster" of *Beowulf*, is described as a two-legged being, considerably larger and stronger than a man, loathsome in appearance and possessing unbelievable strength in his taloned hands. He dwells far off, in a cave in the depths of the forest, approachable only through a fearsome swamp.

No personal pronoun identifies the minor character who provides the emotional impact.

Most shortcuts and tips favor the *dual-pronoun viewpoint* because *you* has become one of the magic words for quick reader identification. Any time you can introduce this word into your piece, you set up direct communication with the reader. Since you may write this

‡Ibid.
§Ibid.

viewpoint several ways, choose the type that best projects your filler or short feature. Remember, projection means transferring your thoughts exactly to the reader.

Many tips or shortcuts imply the *I* who gives the information, and only the *you* appears in the text, as in this one from *Capper's Weekly*.

> If *your* husband uses Borax to clean greasy hands, save the empty cans. Clean the outside, then cover with pretty pieces of contact paper.

By stating the *you*, "your husband," the author focuses immediately on the reader. The shift to the implied *you* for the instructions places the emphasis on the doing.

Some fillers even imply the *you*, as in this example from "Hints From Readers" in *Popular Mechanics*.

> Add height to sawhorses and avoid stooping by clamping a pair of rectangular frames to the top crosspiece. The frame sides should be made the same width as the sawhorse top.—JOHN F. DINGES

This short tip appeared in *Capper's Weekly's* "In the Heart of the Home" section. It states both the *I* and the *you*.

> Does dust from the heavier materials used in macrame bother *you?* Breathing in these fine fibers was really hurting *me*. So I tried putting the loose skeins into the dryer and running it for a while. It took out much of the dust and made the heavier cords easier to work. Do try it.

In the newsbreak, you may find another type of viewpoint, the *editorial we*, as in this example from *AG-Pilot International*.

> The "New" International AG-Pilots Association . . . We understand this new organization has plans for a whole rash of benefits for its members, one being affiliated with the Pilots Lobby, Inc., of Washington, D.C., who have been extremely effective as a pressure group on the hill (much to our benefit).

13

As you can clearly see, this represents the editorial opinion of the specific magazine.

At this point you probably need a suggestion for choosing the best viewpoint. First, you must look at your material and see which viewpoint offers the best projection to the editor and the reader. Then study the magazine where you intend to submit and see which type of viewpoint appears most frequently.

If you find no items written in the viewpoint you chose, substitute the one that appears most frequently. Never suggest to the editors— in any manner whatever—that they use another viewpoint. When you find the editor buys the viewpoint you've selected, then you have taken a forward step in analyzing a market. By all means make a note of this information. An editor may show no preference, so choose the viewpoint that reaches the reader the quickest.

CHARACTERIZATION

Some material, such as anecdotes and short articles, requires mini-characterization of people. Tags offer the best way to do this because they give instant recognition and provide a variety of projections.

1. Action Tag The verb you use to show how the character acts gives the reader an instant picture, as in these three separate examples.

> The gas station attendant *hustled* up to the car.
>
> I *rapped* each melon with my knuckle.
>
> The old lady *tottered* into the bus.

Each of the italicized verbs projects a quick picture of the person. Action can include any movement of the body, facial expression, gesture—to name a few.

2. Speech Tag Speech tags project characters by how they talk. In showing how a person speaks, include the flow of the speech, voice inflections, tone, and choice of words. Study these examples.

"You've never done anything right in your life," she flared. *(words and tone)*

"Hey," the sarge bellowed, "where in the blazes are you going?" *(words, tone, and flow of speech)*

"I'll be switched," he said in amazement. "What brought you here?" *(words, inflection, and emotion)*

3. Background Tag Quite often you project a person by giving his profession, age, organization, or religion, as in these illustrations.

He decided to pay a visit to a beloved *school teacher. (profession)*

My *six-year-old* hunted for his toy train. *(age)*

As *chairman of the PTA,* I read a few lines of inspiration at each meeting. *(organization)*

4. Sensory Tag You may project a character by appealing to the five senses: taste, sight, touch, hearing, and smell. Note the italicized words in these sentences that indicate the sensory.

My child *spit* out the *bitter* medicine. *(taste and sight)*

An exotic *aroma* trailed after the woman. *(smell)*

He *smoothed* the child's *blond curls. (touch and sight)*

The *chirping* voice echoed in my ears. *(hearing)*

5. Mental Tag Thought patterns quickly show a character to the reader.

The woman opened her mouth as if to speak and then shut it. *(insecure thinker)*

The boy stated his opinion in a rapid flow of words. *(quick thinker)*

The man insisted on doing research before he gave an answer. *(methodical thinker)*

In writing any filler or short feature, keep it brief, but at the same time give the reader an adequate picture of the characters. Thus, tags serve as labels and encourage the reader to collaborate and breathe life into characters, individualizing them with imagination. The way you tag characters creates conflict and helps you move on to the humorous ending or serious message. So select your tags carefully and get top mileage from them.

ACTION

You may expand your filler or short feature through a number of different devices. Your material and the market requirements will guide you in selecting the best device. Oddities, newsbreaks, new products, and other similar fillers demand simple narration.

1. Narration With the device of narration, you can cover more information in fewer words. Narration, however, moves slowly and sometimes reads dully, but you can make it quite lively, as in this opening of a mini-article from *People on Parade*.

> Fred Bennetto of North Branford, Conn., isn't one to drop names. He picks them up. Forty-six years ago the famed aviatrix, Amelia Earhart, gave Fred her autograph, and he's been hooked ever since.
> Bennetto's collection contains more than 3,000 signatures and has an estimated value of more than $35,000. Just about every important person is represented in his 35-volume display, says Bennetto. He counts kings, queens, U.S. Presidents, sport heroes, military, Nobel and Pulitzer prize winners among his souvenirs. He says he finds it easier to tell who is missing from his files than to attempt to name those included. . . . —ED WALSH

2. Description Description differs from narration in that you employ imagery and figures of speech to present the action and create a mood. Description dominates this filler called "Hometown Heartbeat" from *Capper's Weekly.*

> Nestled amid tall pine and fir trees, and rolling green fertile countryside, Tualatin, Oregon, is a peaceful sight to behold.

> Situated on the banks of the lazy Tualatin River, the bustling little city is a city within the big city of Portland. . . .
> The countryside is dotted with modern ranch-style homes as well as stately old homes where farm animals graze serenely in the clear air and blue sky. . . . —VERDA RICE

To write this kind of filler, the editor suggests you "consider its [the town's] history, early-day anecdotes, people who have lived there, unique architecture, landmarks, specific crops or industries— that is, write of anything that makes your town distinctive, a place other readers might wish to visit." You can see that to comply with these instructions would require a great deal of description. However, keep the article under 300 words.

3. Explanation Most shortcuts, recipes, tips, or crafts rely on the device of explanation. The writer explains to the reader how to solve a problem, make an item, or save time and effort. A picture may accompany the tip or craft to make the information more graphic. This illustration, "Bobbing Head" by D. A. Woodliff, comes from *Primary Treasure.*‖

> Begin your bobbing head by gluing the spring into the center of the smaller half of the egg-shaped container with epoxy lue. When this has dried and set, glue the other end of the spring into the out- side center of the bigger half on the egg-shaped container. If you don't have a spring to use, cut a small piece of sponge, about 1¼ inches long and about ¾ inch wide, and glue that onto the egg- shaped container in the same way. . . .

The explanation gives simple and specific instructions in a step-by- step procedure.

4. Dramatic Action Narration tells what happens, but dramatic ac- tion shows the event. Select strong action verbs and adverbs to give

‖Copyright © 1979 by Pacific Press Publishing Association. Reprinted by permission.

graphic and exciting pictures. The character tags add emphasis, as in this excerpt from an anecdote in *Reader's Digest*.¶

> A gunman *jumped* out of the bushes at the tenth hole at Cedar Crest Golf Course in Dallas and *demanded* money from the foursome *playing* the hole. They *quietly handed* over their money and *went on* with the game. A caddie, however, *was sent* to the clubhouse to call the police.

The italicized words show the action. The writer takes the reader on scene to experience the action as it happens.

5. Series of Incidents Most fillers and short features take place at one time and one place, but some do happen in more than one period, such as the personal experience, mini-profile, newsbreak, or oddity. If your short feature includes several different time periods, a series of incidents works beautifully. In this device you summarize the problem situation for the reader with a binder sentence and then show the developing action in dialogue or narration according to the various time periods. At the end you briefly state the outcome or result.

Grit, "The Kindest Act" by A. H. Ziegler, provides this illustration.

> I always put out a bird feeder and keep it filled with a variety of seeds for winter birds. *(binder sentence)*
> In *February, 1979*, I was at my kitchen window watching the birds as they feasted at the feeder. Suddenly a cat rushed in and caught a female cardinal.
> I *immediately* ran out and yelled at the cat, which dropped the bird about 20 feet from the feeder.
> On the *fourth day*, I noticed a male cardinal coming to the feeder and carrying seeds to a blue spruce tree in my garden. Upon investigating, I saw the male cardinal actually feeding the female that had been injured. She fluttered her wings like a young bird as he fed her.
> This went on for about *three days*. After that, the female cardinal

recovered enough to come within 10 feet of the feeder, where she would wait until the male fed her.

After *several more days* during which she gained her strength and confidence, she came to the feeder and ate for herself. *(outcome sentence)*

6. Scene Most anecdotes or short personal experiences project the action with a scene. A scene involves conflict between two or more persons at one time and in one place. Generally, you build the scene around the W-words—*where, when, why, who,* and *what,* and conclude with a short *outcome.*

WHERE: In many anecdotes the setting provides a necessary part of the humor.

WHEN: On some occasions the time of the day or the year influences the humor and also promotes reader identification.

WHY: This states the reason for the action.

WHO: A scene requires two or more characters to create the conflict action by showing different views of the situation.

WHAT: One character, the viewpoint, introduces the situation. The other character becomes the opponent. The presentation of this action in several lines of dialogue effectively gives naturalism as well as sparkle to the anecdote or experience.

OUTCOME: In the anecdote, the punch line or the reversal the reader does not expect ends the scene. In a short personal experience, the writer makes a number of decisions that lead to new problems in an effort to find a solution. These various decisions provide the forward action of the experience and lead to a solution.

Let's analyze an example from *Discovery,* the Allstate Motor Club magazine, called "The Bright Side of the Road," by John Johnson.°

Who, When, Where, and Why

On our way through Eastern Tennessee, my wife and I stopped for lunch in a small town that also was the county seat. As I pulled into a space in a crowded parking area in the courthouse square, I asked a uniformed officer if it would be all right to park there.

19

What

"No," he replied.
"But what about all those other cars?" I countered.

Outcome

"They didn't ask," he said.

Writing a good scene depends greatly upon good dialogue. In dialogue you simply apply the techniques of a cameraman in filming a movie or shooting a television script. The camera focuses on the person who will speak. The person speaks. The camera moves over to the next speaker, and he says his part. Once the viewer becomes acquainted with the speakers, the camera brings them on scene together to lead up to the outcome.

In the preceding example the camera would focus on the writer, who then directs the spotlight to the uniformed officer. Then both characters appear on scene for the conflict and the outcome.

The words must characterize the speakers, as do the blunt "no" of the officer and the complaint of the writer. By all means let the *said* project the emotions of the speakers. How the person speaks must relate to the spoken words and action. The officer merely *replies*, and the writer *counters*. The writer has now set the stage for the outcome with a simple *said*.

Make each of these techniques your own so that they will go to work for you when you write your fillers and short features. In fact, you can use some of these techniques when you write short and witty fillers.

3*
Short and Witty

Shakespeare pointed out that "Brevity is the soul of wit." Many fillers depend upon brevity to make the wit or wisdom pay. Do consider wit in its fullest meaning: light and airy, wise and serious, or humorous and delightful. Above all, keep the wit pithy. The following explanations and examples show you how to write wit with a number of many-splendored facets.

FIGURES OF SPEECH

Figures of speech come from a number of sources: published material, radio, television, or movies. In many cases you may create them yourself. If you take figures of speech from any source other than your own imagination, give appropriate credit; some editors pay both the source and the submitter. As previously mentioned, you may need to secure permission in the event the figure of speech you use comes from a book or magazine. To guide yourself in selecting figures of speech by others or creating your own, study these published examples.

1. Personification In personification you endow an inanimate object with human powers. These examples come from "Toward More Picturesque Speech" in *Reader's Digest.*°

> An old fence staggering down the road.—FRANCES FROST

> A parking meter with time on its hands.—MRS. J. T. HENDERSON

° Copyright © 1966 by The Reader's Digest Association, Inc. Reprinted by permission.

> Little hamlets going to sleep, window by window.—MARY C.
> DORSEY

"Flights of Fancy" in *Catholic Digest* published these.

> Windows peeking demurely from under awning eyelashes.—JOHN
> K. YOUNG
>
> Truth shrinking as it stretched.—MRS. E. V. BOE
>
> The moon rode the hills like a pumpkin coach.—PAUL BOWLES

2. Simile A simile compares two similar things or ideas, as in these from "Toward More Picturesque Speech." †

> Tax loopholes are like parking spaces—they all seem to have disappeared by the time you get there.—BILL VAUGHAN
>
> She looked like yesterday's news.—JANE GULICK
>
> Pumpkins lying like fallen suns.—JOSEPH MANTON

"Flights of Fancy" offered these types.

> Fingers twisting like live bait in a jar.—HEDDA HOPPER
>
> Fragments of a smile clung to her lips like cake crumbs.—TRUMAN
> CAPOTE
>
> Untrustworthy as a new bottle of catsup.—GEORGE DEWITT

The words *as* or *like* will help you recognize the simile easily.

3. Metaphor The metaphor equates one thing with another, as in these excerpts from "Toward More Picturesque Speech." ‡

> The good old days, formerly known as these trying times—*Changing Times*

† Ibid.
‡ Ibid.

The difference between an itch and an allergy is about $25.—ROG-ER ALLEN, *Grand Rapid Press*

June is a girl's idea of the perfect end to a marry chase.

"Flights of Fancy" published these metaphors.

Blackbirds displaying patent leather wings.—MRS. E. E. MATIS

Needles of rain stitching together heaven and earth.—SISTER M. IMMACULATE

Petal hands.—KATHLEEN NORRIS

In these examples the authors define the wings as patent leather, the rain as needles, and the hands as petals.

4. Hyperbole The hyperbole deliberately exaggerates for effect or emphasis, as in these selections from "Toward More Picturesque Speech."§

Laugh: a smile that burst.—PATRICIA NELSON

She's been pressing thirty so long it's pleated.—LOUISE A. SAFFRAN

Rooftops shingled with gulls.—KEN G. DALTON, *Enterprise and Times*

He only opens his mouth to change his feet.—MARY L. LYON

The hyperbole appears equally popular with "Flights of Fancy."

A boy glued his hands in prayer.—ART SEIDENBAUM

Deep thoughts wrapped in a corrugated brow.—RICHARD T. JOHNSON

Pounded the table with his voice.—MARY LOETH

He stared past the fire into his thoughts.—JOHN STEINBECK

Eyebrows prying loose an idea.—RICHARD T. JOHNSON

§ Ibid.

5. Pun The pun plays on words that sound alike but have different meanings. These samples come from "Toward More Picturesque Speech." ‖

> A tee-totaler is one who disputes your golf score.—EARL WILSON
>
> Coffee: Break fluid.—MRS. R. R. ANDERSON
>
> Postman's song: "To Each His Zone."—JACK HERBERT, quoted by Earl Wilson

"Flights of Fancy" printed these choices.

> Showed her dislike in no uncertain squirms.—MAURICE SEITTER
>
> Engaged in a tongue of war.—SISTER CESIRA, F.M.A.
>
> Putting problems aside for a brainy day.—JAMES L. SAWYER

6. Imagery Imagery refers to the art of projecting poetic word pictures. These selections appeared in "Toward More Picturesque Speech." ¶

> The Midas touch of fall.—CLARA GILMORE
>
> Harbor confettied with boats.—JIM BISHOP
>
> Driftwood gnarling in the sun.—LESLIE HALL
>
> Leaves sliding down banisters of air.—RALPH W. SEAGER, *Saturday Evening Post*

These examples come from "Flights of Fancy."

> Lightning tearing the sky down the dotted line.—JANE MERCHANT
>
> Mother processing her children for bed.—DOROTHY HOFBAUER
>
> Archipelago of freckles.—RICHARD BISSELL
>
> A zipper of lightning opened a rain-filled sky.—EVELYN L. LESCH

Waves with chrome-plated bumpers.—LEROY J. HERBERT

Perceptive imagination provides the best qualification for recognizing or creating figures of speech that sell.

THE WITTY SENTENCE

One sentence may contain a great deal of wit or wisdom. The markets for these witty and wise sentences require learning definite thought patterns.

1. Epigram Samuel Taylor Coleridge defined the epigram in this way: "A dwarfish whole, its body brevity, and wit its soul." This definition somewhat limits the present-day epigram. Although you must keep the epigram brief and witty, in that you speak and exit quickly, the sentence must also convey instant understanding. If the editor must read the epigram a second time to catch the witticism, it goes into the rejection pile.

The epigram always contains a grain of truth that touches everyday living; consequently, it appeals to a wide group of readers. This appeal may narrow for a specialty magazine which emphasizes, for example, sports or education. So visualize your reader and touch that person's experiences.

Keep the epigram in the realm of good taste. It should belittle recognizable human weaknesses and never sneer at race or physical handicaps. Above all, fit the epigram to the market requirement. If you wish to sell to a special market, read at least six magazine issues containing epigrams. With careful analysis, you will soon learn the thought pattern of the epigram for that special magazine.

Epigrams come from different sources. You may choose the epigram from quotations of famous people, living or deceased, as shown by these examples.

Most people would succeed in small things if they were not troubled by big ambitions.—HENRY WADSWORTH LONGFELLOW

The great pleasure a dog is, is that you may make a fool of yourself with him and not only will he not scold you, but he will make a fool of himself, too.—SAMUEL BUTLER

It is well for the heart to be naive and for the mind not to be. —ANATOLE FRANCE, in "Quotable Quotes," *Reader's Digest*°

Experience keeps a dear school, but fools still learn in no other. —BENJAMIN FRANKLIN

The mass media—television, radio, movies, and newspapers—may supply epigrams.

A sweater is a garment that a child wears when his mother feels chilly.—SAM LEVENSON, on "The Mike Douglas Show"

Is there anything more embarrassing than jumping at a conclusion that isn't there?—EARL WILSON, in "Quotable Quotes," *Reader's Digest* †

The writer may adapt a well-known epigram by reversing the thought, or by only reconditioning it to make it topical. A mere substitution of words can result in a parody, pun, or reversal, as in these selections from several magazines.

Look for a blessing that's not in disguise.—JEAN KERR, in "Flights of Fancy"

He was born with a silver spoon in his mouth and hasn't stirred since.—HERB SCHRINER, *Reader's Digest* ‡

One good turn gets more of the blanket.—"Toward More Picturesque Speech," *Reader's Digest* §

In any good household, junk accumulates to fill the space available for its storage.—BRUCE O. BOSTON, in "Along the Shore," *Knowledge News Features*

Folks usually call a person dumb simply because he's smart about the wrong things.—"Talelights," *Grit*

Some high-rollers play golf as if their wives depended on it!—JEAN FERRIS, in "Rub of the Grin," *Golf Digest*

A great oak is only a little nut that held its ground.—GLADYS HASH FELICE, in *Good Housekeeping* ‖

A girl with money to burn has no trouble finding a match.—C.M.A., in *Good Housekeeping* ¶

Between marbles, courtship, and crabgrass, a man spends half of his life on his knees!—*Humorama, Inc.* °

Reformers are usually members of the meddle class.—JACK HERBERT, in "Parting Shots," *The American Legion Magazine* †

Love is the stamp of a "real" parent.—"Suzie," in *Midnight/Globe*

A careful study of these examples will guide you in meeting the qualifications of a salable epigram.

Once you get the feel of the epigram, you will create your own. Begin by listing subjects with strong reader identification: love, happiness, marriage, money, truth, or inflation. Think of something you can say about any of these which warns against a human weakness but remains timely. All of us have told a white lie to keep from doing something or going someplace. Then we can't remember exactly what excuse we gave. Let's write this situation into an epigram: "He who tells the truth today need not test his memory tomorrow."

Take inflation. Since some people buy as long as credit lasts, we might say: "Inflation is the companion of those who spend freely." We can put this more tersely: "Credit today and bankruptcy tomorrow." Why not stop right here and try your hand at writing an epigram?

2. Quip The quip consists of an epigram served with a humorous comment. You frustrate expectations with a reversal in thought. The

---

‖Copyright © 1967 by The Hearst Corporation. Reprinted by permission.
¶ Ibid.
° Copyright © 1967 by Humorama, Inc. Reprinted by permission.
† Copyright © 1967 by The American Legion Magazine. Reprinted by permission.

quip must meet the same requirements as the epigram: brevity, clearness, reader identification, and instant wit.

The quip also comes from the same sources as the epigram: a playback from what a stand-up comedian says, an ad-lib, or a seemingly spur-of-the-moment comment in a movie. Look for quips in newspapers, magazines, or books. As a final source, listen to comments of friends; when one person remarks on a reader-identification situation and another retorts, jot this down in your notebook as you do sources of other quips.

The quip may need only a single sentence for expression. These selections come from "Parting Shots" in *The American Legion Magazine*.‡

> If you want to sign something that will last forever, sign a mortgage.—GEORGE DELAINE
>
> The girl who loves and loses probably didn't have the right lawyer.—EDWARD OTTO

"Talelights" in *Grit* published these quips.

> The hardest part about doing nothing is you don't know when you finish.
>
> Cross the bridges before you come to them, and you have to pay the toll twice.
>
> The trouble with self-service gas stations is they clean your wallet, but not your windshield.

"Along the Shore" from *Knowledge News Features* printed these.

> In matters of dispute, the bank's balance is always smaller than yours.—ROZANNE WEISMAN
>
> You can observe a lot just by watching.—YOGI BERRA

‡ Copyright © 1979 by The American Legion Magazine. Reprinted by permission.

The quip may define or compare, as in these samples from *Good Housekeeping.* §

> Gossip is like a snapshot: it begins with a negative, has been developed and is often enlarged. —JEAN LEEDALE KNIGHT

> There isn't much to be seen in a little town, but what you hear makes up for it. —KIN NUBBARD

"Quotable Quotes" from *Reader's Digest* published these. ‖

> One revolution is just like one cocktail—it gets you organized for the next. —WILL ROGERS

> We can easily forgive a child who is afraid of the dark; the real tragedy of life is when men are afraid of the light. —PLATO

> It seems that everything today is wrinkle-resistant except people. —NORMAN E. MOORE, in *The Saturday Evening Post*

This quip comes from "Parting Shots" in *The American Legion Magazine.* ¶

> Bankruptcy is when a man's yearning capacity exceeds his earning capacity and his creditor's lending capacity. —WILFRED BEAVER

Humorama, Inc. contributed this quip. °

> Nature didn't make us perfect, so she did the next best thing, she made us blind to our own faults.

I found this quip in "Dear Suzie" in *Midnight/Globe.*

> Crime wouldn't pay if the government ran it. —MICHAEL D. HERTZ

The quip may need two sentences for full development, as in these selections, also from "Dear Suzie."

> The hardest part of dieting is not watching what you eat. It's watching what your friends eat.—ROY LAIRMORE

> The hardest lesson in life is to learn to be yourself. Sure it's easier to conform, but it's more satisfying to be faithful to your beliefs. —ANNMARIE JONES

Good Housekeeping used this quip with the two-sentence format.†

> I'm tired of fair-weather friends. What I want is a rain beau. —EDITH OGUTSCH

This two-sentence quip appeared in "Quotable Quotes" in *Reader's Digest.*‡

> Things tend to even up. The more bodily weight you carry around, the shorter time you're likely to carry it.

Orben's Current Comedy and *Orben's Comedy Fillers* contributed these examples.§

> Cheap? Let's just say he goes in for no-frills tipping.

> Santa Claus is the one who's making a list and checking it twice— he's gonna find out who's naughty and nice. So are the voters.

> There's one big problem with a do-it-yourself project. Who do you blame?

Basically, to write a quip start with a truism or adage about a subject which touches a wide group of people. Take money as an

---

example. Suppose we say that money doesn't bring happiness. This accepted truth touches everyone's life.

To comment on it you try to think of the average person's reaction to money—he or she would like to have more of it. So let's say something which shows this attitude in the quip: "Money doesn't always bring happiness, but it supports you while you look."

You can phrase this quip in another way: "Some things are bigger than money—" Now to quip you add: "like mortgages," "like down payments on houses," or "like debts."

Learn now that you don't dash off a quip. Instead you revise and polish, put aside for a while, and then do more work. With the right kind of practice, however, you can quip with the experts.

3. Definition In developing the thought pattern of a daffy definition, you define a word used in everyday living, such as *bachelor, tact, teen-ager, wig, sailor,* or *happiness.* Make a list of words you commonly hear as you go through your daily routine. Next define the selected words in terms of human action or reaction.

Take the aging process. A friend of mine gave her husband a self-winding watch, but it kept stopping on him. The salesperson insisted the trouble resulted from the husband's inactivity and asked his age. This formed the basis of a good definition. "Age: when your self-winding watch doesn't wind." This defines age in timely action.

The pun can make a daffy definition more humorous. "Toward More Picturesque Speech," in *Reader's Digest,*‖ published these.

Disinherit: hair brush.—AL BERNSTEIN

Freudian slip: id skid.—JEAN FARRIS

Bathing beauty: a girl worth wading for.—GENERAL FEATURES CORPORATION

Orben's Comedy Fillers gives this definition with a pun.¶

‖Copyright © 1965, 1966 by The Reader's Digest Association, Inc. Reprinted by permission.

¶Copyright © 1979 by Robert Orben. Reprinted by permission.

New Year's Eve is when you get a new lush on life.

A definition may utilize a reversal, as in these selections from "Toward More Picturesque Speech" in *Reader's Digest.*°

> Sympathy: what one girl offers in exchange for details.
>
> Teen-ager: one who has reached the age of dissent.—HAROLD D. LESLIE

Any definition requires a clever twist of words. Let's look at a few examples from various magazines.

> Charge account: the lie-awake plan.—ALBERT MANSKI, in "Flights of Fancy," *Catholic Digest*
>
> Duck hunters: what ducks try to do.—RAYMOND J. COIKOTA, in *Good Housekeeping†*
>
> Divorce: a condition brought on by two people who were crazy to get married.—P. TONY PETTITO, in "Parting Shots," *The American Legion Magazine‡*
>
> Work is the recreation of the retired.—*Orben's Current Comedy§*

Discipline yourself to develop the thinking patterns of the definition. Never feel satisfied with the first effort, but write five or six and choose only the best. Test your definitions on your family or friends and see if they laugh. Don't tell the definitions, but ask them to read them from the paper where you typed them. Remember, when you recite them, you add facial expression and voice tone you do not put on the paper. The humor must stand on its own.

4. Signs Collecting signs typical of everyday life tests your powers of observation. You already know where to look for them, so now you must learn how to write them. You always give the place, for this often creates the humor. The sign has a wide market, as seen in these selections.

> In the window of a barber shop: "If you don't like the looks of your heir, send him to us."—LANE OLINGHOUSE, in *Good Housekeeping*‖

> In an oculist's window: "We correct everything in sight."—MRS. S. LEE, in "Signs of the Times," *Catholic Digest*

> Sign outside an auto repair shop: "Secondhand cars in first-crash condition."—BENNET CERF, in "Toward More Picturesque Speech," *Reader's Digest*¶

A pun, as in a definition, adds humor to the sign.

> Sign on a honeymoon car: "Till draft do us part."—RAILWAY CARMEN, in "Toward More Picturesque Speech," *Reader's Digest*°

> At a chicken farm: "Cheepers by the dozen."—MRS L. BINDER, in "Signs of the Times," *Catholic Digest*

You may coin words, as Gil Stern did in this example from "Parting Shots" in *The American Legion Magazine.*†

> There's a sign on a girl's closet in a nearby sorority house which reads: "No dresspassing."

The sign may exhibit a bit of philosophy, as in these three selections.

> Posted on a school bulletin board: "During examination periods the ruling against prayer on school premises is temporarily suspended."—JACK HERBERT, in *Good Housekeeping*‡

In a small West Texas café: "The banker has agreed that if I won't cash any checks, he won't sell any chili."—MARY G. TSCHIDE, in "Signs of the Times," *Catholic Digest*

Savings & Loan billboard: "We not only pay dividends. We show interest."—WALLACE MCGUIRE, in "Toward More Picturesque Speech," *Reader's Digest* §

Interest has developed in guide posters at churches. *Guideposts* published these two examples.‖

"Failure is the line of least persistence."—seen outside the First Congregational Church, Binghamton, New York

"Seven days without prayer makes one weak."—Ferguson Avenue Baptist Church, Chatham County, Georgia

Test the signs you see and determine if they will interest an editor. Editors can tell you if they find them truly amusing.

PRESS ERRORS

Perhaps you have noticed typographical errors in your newspaper. These imperfections form the basis of another humorous filler.

1. News Slips The typographical error can change the entire meaning of a sentence. One letter makes a great deal of difference, as in these selections published in *Reader's Digest.*¶

From a report on a new college dormitory in the Lansing (Michigan) *State Journal:* "It will house 120 men in one tower and 120 women in the other with a common lunge area."

From the Mansfield (Ohio) *News-Journal:* "He was sent to sea to learn its hardships. Instead he learned to love the sailor's wife."

This amusing example comes from "Short Takes" in *Editor & Publisher*.

> "The three major hospitals participating in the program are being asked to donate at a rate of $10 per dead."—San Rafael (California) *Independent-Journal*

Note the difference in the two markets. *Reader's Digest* uses an introductory phrase and the source while *Editor & Publisher* lets the error stand alone and then gives the source.

2. Advertisements Humor in an advertisement comes from employing the wrong words, as in this excerpt from *Reader's Digest*.°

> Ad in an Alabama newspaper: "Internationally known stylist Mr. Andre will be at Sonya House of Beauty for consolations on hair coloring and styling."

The arrangement of the words frequently makes a filler of this type humorous. This often occurs in the classified section, where people try to say something briefly to save on the cost of the ad. *Good Housekeeping* purchased this error.†

> Wanted: Girls to play ragtime piano. Don't have to be good.— Phoenix (Arizona) *Republic*, from "Addle Ads," submitted by Juliet Lowell

If this type of filler appeals to you, begin at once to train your eye to catch these errors in the press. Keep your scissors handy and snip.

LIGHT VERSE

Light verse requires a major effort because you must create humor in two to four lines of rhyme. But when you consider the great demand for these rhymes, you should try writing some verse. Any-

° Ibid.
† Copyright © 1967 by The Hearst Corporation. Reprinted by permission.

one who has a sense of humor and a feeling for rhyme and rhythm can sell this market by following these few basic rules.

Like other short fillers, the verse needs a universal appeal or reader-identification subject. The more people who can identify with the situation described in your verse, the more opportunity you have to sell. So transfer your frustrations, human failings, or slight protests to verse. This verse comes from *Home Life*.

> Summer's here and school is done
> The kids look forward to months of fun;
> Trips to enjoy and to remember,
> Lord, help me survive until September
> —BOBBIE HANSON

Keep the poem short, making every word count, but give your reader a well-rounded thought, as in this couplet from "Parting Shots" by Rosemarie Williamson in *The American Legion Magazine*. ‡

Saturday's Child
> Every fall the same old image—
> Pretzels, beer and line of scrimmage!

The following couplets appeared in *Good Housekeeping*. §

> What makes a waiter a total wreck?
> Eight women splitting a luncheon check.
> —DOROTHY BENNETT

Population Figures
> They're easy to see
> On mothers-to-be.
> —BERT KRUSE

Don't try to invent new forms, but rely on the established couplet or quatrain. Occasionally, a magazine will use a limerick. In a qua-

---

‡ Copyright © 1979 by The American Legion Magazine. Reprinted by permission.
§ Copyright © 1967 by The Hearst Corporation. Reprinted by permission.

train, preferably rhyme the first and third lines and the second and fourth, as in this selection from *Golf Digest*.

Counterbalanced

Whenever I'm hitting 'em straight off the tee
You can bet that it's not by the book.
The reason, indeed, is more likely to be
That I'm putting a slice in my hook.

—MRS. LILLIAN HERMAN

Many quatrains, however, rhyme only the second and the fourth lines, so choose the form most natural for you. *Golf Digest* published this example.

Don't Do It, Detroit!

I live in fear that, some grim year,
All autos will have shrunk
To where a fellow cannot get
His clubs into the trunk.

—DICK EMMONS

The title provides an additional humorous touch to the verse. It must fit the thought in the rhyme but not betray the reversal. Remember, the editor sees the title first, so make it as eye-catching as you can. Puns make good titles, but sometimes long, rambling titles work well for very short couplets. Study the titles on the examples already quoted.

The family pet may inspire a humorous verse. This example appeared in *Discovery*.

The Purrfect Spot

Piles of laundry, clean and sweet,
Freshly ironed shirt and sheet,
These are what our cat prefers
To lie upon and say his purrs!

—JEANNE WESTERDALE

The verse should always end with a humorous punch line; so completely reverse the original premise whenever possible. The more surprising the funnier, as in this one from *Orben's Comedy Fillers*.‖

> Words take many meanings,
> In truth as well as jibe;
> What ads proclaim a rebate—
> Was once just called a bribe.

Note the reversal in this verse by Stephen Schlitzer in "Parting Shots" from *The American Legion Magazine*.¶

> Cooking at my outdoor grill
> Is fraught with risk and tedium
> I usually get my steaks quite rare
> My hands and fingers medium.

Some editors buy short verses with a serious thought, too, like this example from *Grit* in a section called "Poetry Just for You."

February, 1980

> Dividing the current year by four,
> We find that there is one day more
> In which to laugh, and love, and live;
> To feel compassion, to forgive.
>
> —FRANK FILLERY

A sense of rhythm and rhyme helps in writing verse. A knack for finding a new way to say the same old thing also makes a plus. So give your verse the singsong of iambic feet and add a dash of rhyme to cloak your thoughts. Keep the reader identification strong.

Perhaps you would like to stop right here and try some figures of speech, a witty sentence, a verse or two. If these fillers fail to inspire you, you may find tips and shortcuts more to your liking.

‖Copyright © 1979 by Robert Orben. Reprinted by permission.

¶Copyright © 1966 by The American Legion Magazine. Reprinted by permission.

4*
Tips and Shortcuts

When a task around the house or in your shop takes too long, you endeavor to find a quicker and more efficient way of handling the problem. A tip or shortcut briefly but clearly explains a practical way of saving time, money, and energy when solving a knotty problem. Usually, tips either originate from your own experience or someone you know passes them on.

Too frequently you keep your knowledge to yourself in spite of the fact that many magazines will pay you to share your information. No doubt, many of you have read a published handy tip and said to yourself, "But I've been doing that for years." You failed to put it on paper and submit it to the most likely market.

Perhaps you lack confidence in your tip or, more likely, in your ability to write it clearly and concisely. Nothing gives you more confidence than knowing exactly how to get the tip on paper.

TIP PATTERN

The specific pattern for the tip varies with the market and the material, as does the viewpoint. Once you know the general arrangement, you can study the market for the particular pattern before you submit. Keep the tip brief—within fifty words if possible. A few magazines will allow more words.

1. **Problem** In the opening sentence you introduce the tip with a bit of salesmanship by telling the reader how this information will save him time. You might relate how you discovered it if the maga-

zine allows that many words. This example comes from "Crosscuts" in *Workbench,* under shop tips.

Problem

An empty coffee can with a plastic lid can save your paint brushes and wasted solvent.

2. Solution Although these tips generally appear in one sentence or a paragraph, you can see definite steps in presenting the information. In this second step you blueprint the information so that the reader may follow it to the word. This may take considerable rewriting until you master the art of brevity and clarity. Let's continue with the second part of the illustration.

Solution

Make a 2½-inch slit across the center of a three-pound coffee-can lid. When you want to soak a brush, fill a small can wider than the brush, and place in the bottom of the larger can. Slide the handle through the slotted lid and adjust the brush so only the bristles are in the solvent.

3. Result Some magazines stop with the solution, while others devote a sentence cautioning against pitfalls or encouraging the reader with the beneficial results. This example stresses the beneficial results.

Results

This not only saves solvent, but eliminates bent bristles too.

The two-step pattern combines either the problem and the solution or the solution and the result. To determine which pattern to use, decide which will best show your material. Then study the magazine to see which pattern appears most frequently in print.

In a very short form that appears occasionally, you can write the tip in one sentence, as Mrs. W. Frank did for "Dear Suzie" in *Midnight/Globe.*

Use talcum powder to revive old, sticky playing cards.

Choose simple words and short sentences. Some magazines would like a picture or sketch to clarify the solution. Don't worry if your sketch looks rough, for the magazine has a staff artist who can convert it to a professional drawing if necessary. Do make the sketch clear. If you use a photograph, make it sharp enough for the black and white to reproduce clearly. Rarely do you send a color photograph, but check the magazine for the possibility. Some markets require an eight- by ten-inch black-and-white photograph, while others will accept five- by seven-inch snapshots.

When you send a tip from friends, have them check your copy for accuracy as a necessary precaution. Keep this basic organization for a tip in mind when you analyze individual markets.

TIPS FOR WOMEN

Tips for women discuss cleaning house, sewing, cooking, child rearing, or anything that makes work around the home easy. Remember, a salable tip must save money, time, and energy.

Most tips for women run very short, from fifty to two hundred words. If you can write the tip in one sentence, all the better. In short, you compress the three steps of the pattern into one or two sentences. Most tips use the dual-pronoun viewpoint, stressing the implied *I* and *you* for the longer ones. Choose as your viewpoint the one which best projects the information to the reader.

1. Confession Market The pattern for the confession magazines varies from one to three sentences, depending on the tip. The viewpoint consists of the stated or implied *you* as determined by the tip.

The editors of these magazines emphasize that they want practical tips which originate with the readers and not "tired old ones" which have been "making the rounds" for several years with all the magazines. They encourage spontaneous tips motivated by the opportunity to share with other readers.

2. Home Service Magazines These magazines for women of all ages want tips that relate to the home arts of cooking, decorating, and sewing. Tips for these magazines deviate very little in pattern from those for the confession market.

Mrs. Carl Byrd sold this tip to "Reader's Idea Exchange" in *Family Circle.*°

Problem

I like to use fabric-softener sheets for the dryer several times, but because they're so lightweight they end up a mess in the lint catcher.

Solution

Now I pin each new one to an old washcloth and toss that into the dryer with each load until the softener sheet is used up.

Result

The extra weight keeps it out of the lint catcher.

This section also uses the two-step pattern.

The editor at *Family Circle* cautioned, "We get tons of filler submissions which we don't use. Warn your readers to check the market before submission."

"Around the House" in *Good Housekeeping* individualizes the pattern by including the editor's viewpoint and interweaving the names of the contributors. This style makes the column read with the chattiness of talking to a person while sharing a tip during a coffee break from housework, as in this example.†

Problem

In a home with wall-to-wall carpeting, where there's no place for kids to play with games that require a hard surface (to set up building blocks, car or train set), a piece of plywood may be the answer.

Solution

[The mother] bought a piece, small enough to fit under her son's bed, and finished off the edges.

Result

He can slide it in and out anytime he wants.

The editor of this section offers this advice: "I try to use original *ideas* in my column, which I usually rewrite. The 'professional' fillers I receive (with self-addressed, stamped envelope, word count, etc.) are very seldom usable, since they most often have appeared many times in other places, or are old wives' tales. I need the kind of inspired thoughts and ideas that come from 'front line' housekeepers, mothers, fathers and probably nonprofessional writers." By all means follow her advice, as other editors would strongly agree with her.

In submitting to this editor, write your tip briefly but clearly, and she will adapt it to the column. Do take the tip from your own experiences or that of a knowledgeable person.

Better Homes and Gardens features "Tips, Tools & Techniques" designed to make household jobs easier. It includes "shop hints, installation tips, and repair shortcuts" you have experienced "as a do-it-yourselfer," the note from the editor suggests. This market does not accept previously published ideas.

To write for this market, you divide the tip into *problem* and *solution*. Include these two words as headings for the parts of the tip. A sketch may accompany the tip.

3. National Weeklies "Thrift Tip" in *Grit* published this one by Cathie Screnock.

Problem

Use empty shortening cans, coffee cans, or other cylindrical containers as gift containers for cookies.

Solution

Cover the outside with appropriate paper and ribbon.

Result

These containers are particularly handy if you want to send cookies through the mail. The plastic lid which comes with the can keeps the cookies fresh.

Midnight/Globe printed this hint in "Dear Suzie," subtitled "Home Hints." It follows the one-sentence pattern.

Add three parts of oil and one part vinegar to a nearly empty ketchup bottle for a spicy salad dressing.—MRS. E. O'BRIEN

This tip comes from *Capper's Weekly*, "In the Heart of the Home."

Problem and Solution

To save on shampoo, dilute the water half and half, add 1 tablespoon gelatin to control tangles, ½ teaspoon lemon juice or ¼ cup stale beer to make dull hair shine. Cologne can be added for scent.

Caution

Buy the cheapest brand you can, it will get your hair just as clean.

4. Specialty Markets These magazines publish tips and shortcuts that relate to their special readers' interests. The pattern varies with the tip, as does the dual-pronoun viewpoint.

Under "Kitchen Helpers" in *The National Supermarket Shopper*, one person may send in a group of tips in the short form presented here.

Run hot tap water over limes and lemons, then roll them on the counter. They'll give twice as much juice!

Budget sachet: dried orange peels in old nylon stockings on hangers in your closet. Provides a pleasant scent and keeps the moths away.

Insulated ice cream bags are great for storing vegetables or fruit. Produce will remain fresh for a longer period.—MRS. ELISE BREENEN

"Many Other Mother Suggestions" in *Baby Talk* wants any tips that will solve an everyday problem for the nursery set. If you study the magazine, which you can find at the office of a pediatrician or a gynecologist, you'll see that the pattern depends upon the difficulty of the tip. This one by S. LoCastra explains the tip in two sentences.

Problem and Solution

Instead of moving buttons up on the straps of too-long coveralls, just sew on extra buttons at the correct length for now.

Result

When baby grows, you won't have to move them—just snip them off, and the original buttons are still there at the longer length.

McCall's, under the title of "Survival in the Suburbs" asks readers to contribute their ideas on how to solve problems in various living areas. Follow this typical example. ‡

Problem

An estimated 1,000 people move to the booming Houston area each week; many of these newcomers, expecting to see cowboys and tumbleweeds, go into culture shock at the sight of freeways and skyscrapers.

Solution

They can speed their adjustment with a series of courses called "Living in Texas" at Rice University's Department of Continuing Studies. The classes, which began nearly two years ago, explain the Texas way of life, from music to politics.

Result

Although the series was designed specifically for new arrivals, says its originator, Professor Mary McIntyre, half the enrollees have been native Texans. Colleges in Colorado, California and Arkansas have been in touch with her about setting up similar programs.

Under the heading of "Parents' Exchange," *Parent's Magazine* publishes tips that help make life easier for a parent. These follow the three-step pattern but emphasize relations between parents and children.

Tips under "Neighbors" in *Woman's Day* focus on family living. To give you an idea of the subjects covered, read three issues of the section and list the problem in each tip. State your problem, give the solution, and then tell the the happy results. The length varies with the shared tip. The "Neighbors" column dates back to 1938 and rates as the oldest continuing feature in *Woman's Day.* "We look

‡ From "Right Now—Survival in the Suburbs," November, 1979. Reprinted by permission of the McCall Publishing Company.

for submissions from readers who have an idea or experience to share," wrote the editor.

Family Pet Magazine buys tips and shortcuts relating to the care of pets for "Pet Tips." These run between 100 and 450 words.

Quilt World uses the title "Granny Sez" for its tips on quilting. Anne Wittels wrote her tip in verse.§

Problem and Solution
When you put away quilts that you've made
For your kids, or as gifts, or to trade,
Just be sure: SIGN AND DATE.

Result
When they're gone it's too late
Even good quilters' memories fade!

From *Doll World Omnibook* comes this humorous tip in verse by Jen Kost.¶

I've a brand new kitchen
That is "new pin" neat. . . .
That's how I aim to keep it.
We'll dine out, or we can't eat.

As you read the magazines of your choice, you will find other markets that buy tips. Analyze them for subjects, patterns, viewpoint, and style of presentation.

TIPS FOR MEN

The men's market favors the short pattern for the tip but adds a picture or a diagram for clarity. The addition of a photograph increases the payment. Generally, the title on the filler suggests the tip.

1. **Science Magazines** *Popular Mechanics* buys workshop or home-repair tips for "Hints from Readers." This example by Ken

§ Reprinted by permission of the House of the White Birches, Inc., Seabrook, N.H.
¶Ibid.

Patterson appeared in the section under the title of "Light Bulb Replacement Tool."

Problem and Solution

When attached to the end of a broomstick or rod, the spring bulb-clip from a table lamp can replace light bulbs in hard-to-reach places.

Caution

Pad the clip with electrician's tape.

This example by H. E. Moody shows you the very short pattern of the tip, titled "Square Becomes Scriber."

Since I often use my combination square as a marker scriber, I filed a notch in one end of the ruler for the pencil.

A photograph provides a visual detail.

This magazine also purchases "Photo Hints." This one by Bob Berger is titled "Off the Wall."

Problem

Slow shutter speeds require use of a tripod, but often a tripod takes too long to set up or isn't tall enough.

Solution

Try bracing it unextended against a wall;

Result

the camera will be supported as rigidly as if the tripod were on the floor.

A photograph showed this wall brace in use.

Under "Tips & Techniques," *Popular Electronics* publishes technical fillers such as this one by Gane Wong, titled "Cleaning PC Boards."

Problem

The next time you have to clean a printed circuit board, try a scouring pad marketed under the trade name Scotch-Brite.

47

Solution

These green, nonmetallic pads can clean boards (or pots and pans) as effectively as steel wool, but don't rust or splinter, and are kinder to your hands.

Result

In fact, one well-known company includes in its pc etching kit a small pad for cleaning boards which closely resembles the product suggested here.

In these magazines, instead of the happy result, the last sentence often tells where to find the product or promises an easier job next time. Your material will indicate which information to include.

Popular Science has found a unique but very visual way to give the tip, under the title of "Wordless Workshop." Sixteen frames, similar to those in a comic strip, show the action involved in the tip. The first four frames open with the idea of getting the supplies and starting to work. The next four show failures and getting a new idea. The following four depict the steps of the tip. The final four frames picture the tip in operation. Study this tip in at least six issues before you submit, then try to visualize the sixteen frames as you write the tip. Do not submit sketches.

Under the title of "Taking Care of Your Car," the tip from this same magazine follows the long pattern, giving the problem, solution, and results. A sketch makes the tip more graphic. The editor may use your sketch or have it re-drawn.

2. Craft and Shop Tips *Make It With Leather,* under "Tips & Hints," uses illustrations with a pattern comparable to that followed by *Better Homes and Gardens.* Ron Flinsch contributed this tip. Include the words *The Problem* and *The Answer* in the submittal, as shown.

The Problem: Trying to put fine detail into your carvings.

The Answer: Use a hard (5-H) lead pencil.

"Shop Tips" in *Workbench* focuses on woodworking, home improvements, or do-it-yourselfing. In this same general section,

"Reader Service" may pay you for giving answers to readers' inquiries. Jay Knapp submitted this one.

Problem

Noted the problem of F.F. of Middleborough, New York, in the July–August 1977 issue regarding finding that dowels were available only in 36-in. lengths.

I had a similar problem where I needed four 20-in. dowels and was going to have to buy the dowels at $1.25 each and waste 16 in. of each one.

Solution

My solution was to buy an oak handle 7 ft. long at a hardware store. Got the four pieces from the one dowel for $1.89. The handle was a bit over 1 in. in diameter, so the idea will work only where diameter is not critical.

Under "Handy Hints" the *Family Handyman Magazine* shares the best ideas from other readers that will save money and effort on projects all around the home. Write them in the two-sentence pattern and send along sketches or pictures to show results. These hints deal with saving paint, removing bolts and screws, starting screws, or shortcuts in paneling joints, to name a few.

Under "Farm and Shop Ideas," *Farm Journal* publishes tips on homemade gadgets that will save time and labor. A photograph shows the gadget or shortcut the person has invented, so originality and inventiveness pay dividends here. The tip follows the long pattern.

3. Other Markets *Sports Afield* unites a wide variety of tips in "The Sports Afield Almanac." The two-sentence pattern dominates most tips. Study this example on fishing.

Problem

If your fishing time is limited, then pick the two best hours of the day.

Solution

These are the hour beginning with dawn and the hour before dusk—the times when the bigger fish are on the prowl.

49

From this same section comes this rather unusual tip titled "Outdoor Treasures," by Gil Paust.

Problem

An outdoorsman's trips most often take him into the boondocks, the remotest parts of our rural countryside not yet trampled by modern civilizations, and historians remind us that these are the only remaining areas, outside of antique shops and museums, where there still are traces of Early America—old decoys, Kentucky rifles, ancient fishing tackle, pot-belly stoves, kerosene lamps, old bottles and glassware, china, paintings, flags, rag rugs and numerous valuable and still useful items.

Solution

Here the outdoorsman can find historical memorabilia that in the Atlantic States sometimes predates even the Declaration of Independence.

Result

A few hours spent searching for them will not be a waste of time. Some may be too large to fit in his pocket, but are worth a return trip by car.

With a little searching you will find that you, too, have tips you can share with readers.

TIPS FOR MEN AND WOMEN

A number of markets buy tips for both men and women. Some tips slant for the woman, while others cater to the man. A few appeal to both, such as *Guideposts*.

1. **Religious** *Guideposts* wants tips that show how to grow spiritually, in or out of church, for the section titled "Why Don't We?" °

Problem

Here's something you might want to do in your church—a "Talent Trade."

A group of us in our small mission church were discussing Matthew 25:15, and we started thinking about our own talents, however small, and how they could be better used for the Lord.

Solution

Today we have a master list of such things as cake decorating and typing and pottery-making. We offer these talents "for hire." Anybody, say, who wants a particularly beautiful birthday cake can hire our "talented" cake decorator, and then make a reasonable fee-donation to our church. You'd be surprised how needed these little skills and services are. For instance, one mother used to think it an imposition to ask me to stay with her small son when she went out. Now, when she can give to the church, she doesn't mind using my special talent for baby-sitting.

Result

There are God-given talents in your church going to waste. Put them to work—and return His gift to you with interest.—COLLETTA L. NELSON

2. Syndicates The Mike LeFan Syndicate asks for a "Money Saver of the Week and/or Month" that deals with savings on clothes, cars, food, gifts, recreation, homes, and other aspects of daily living. "All fillers," Mike LeFan points out, "must relate to the more-for-your-money theme and be practical." This example slants toward the woman.

Problem and Solution

Mary Champion says, "Never throw away a box of detergent without first rinsing out the box with warm water."

Result

"You will be amazed how many suds are left in the box, enough for one more sinkful of dishes."

The Mother Earth News, under the title of "Mother's Down-Home Country Lore," publishes tips for men and women on catching chickens, tree cutting, preserving elderberries, using soda-can flip tops for picture hangers, waxing hardwood floors, cleaning windows—you name it. The editor blends these tips into interesting reading with a folksy style, as in this example.

Problem

"Have you ever knitted a sweater . . . only to have one arm turn out longer than the other?" asks Laura Hendricks.

Solution

"There's an easy way to insure that both pieces of anything you make in pairs—mittens, sleeves, booties, etc.—will be of equal size. Simply use a long needle . . . and knit two sleeves (or whatever) at the same time."

This tip helps the farm-dwelling reader of the same magazine.

Problem

Roy Millsap's father was tired of trying to catch scampering chickens, so the Oakdale, Connecticut, homesteader devised his very own "elusive-egg-layer nabber."

Solution

He simply took a six-foot length of stiff wire and bent it into this shape. [Sketch shows a hook]

The bird's scrawny leg slips easily into the hook's opening . . . but the fowl's long toes keep it from pulling free.

Result

So nowadays, when the senior Millsap wants a "Sunday dinner special," he just grabs his nabber, traipses out to the flock . . . and snares his meal.

The style of writing creates the impression of the editor talking with the reader. "We're interested in practical, down-home, time-tested solutions to the frustrating little problems that bug us every day," the editor summarizes, "yet we're always overstocked on this kind of information."

Modern Maturity publishes "Tips Worth Considering" to help senior citizens, such as how to buy safety toys for their grandchildren, keep warm in a cold house, watch out for fraud, or use medicine wisely. The section usually lists sources for further research.

So you see, tips range from the very simple to the highly specialized and technical. If you have difficulty making your tip conform to the requirements of a particular market, try this simple expedient. Take scissors and cut the tip apart according to the compressed, short, or long pattern. If you can do this simple analysis, you can easily overlay your tip on the pattern.

The real difficulty in selling a tip lies within the individual who too readily assumes that everyone already knows the information. In any case, a postage stamp and a little effort will give you the answer. You may protest that you do not fit the do-it-yourself profile. Then develop a sense for the unusual newsbreak. Take a pair of scissors and clip your fillers from other published sources. Make sure you credit the source.

*5
Brief and Factual

The brief and factual filler requires accurate research in addition to knowledge of what will catch and hold the interest of the average or specialty-magazine reader. Research consists of two kinds: *primary*, in which you contact the person involved directly or witness the action yourself; or *secondary*, in which you secure the facts from published sources.

As to knowing the interests of readers, you learn this primarily by reading fillers that have already been published and by talking with people. Often you can test the interest of a news item on your bridge or poker group by tossing the odd bit or fact into the conversation during a break and gauging the reaction.

Ignore the group's special interest, but do not select material out of the general public's range. For example, a bridge or poker group would most likely enjoy facts about unusual plays or techniques but show little interest in strange customs of natives in a remote area of Africa. Yet such unusual behavior would interest many readers.

When you snip items from a newspaper, bulletin, advertising pamphlet, or magazine, choose those that center on odd or humorous actions. Remember, readers identify primarily with people.

Some editors want only the original clipping, while others will accept a photocopy or condensed version. Since you cannot always tell from reading the magazine whether the editor or the writer condenses the newsbreak, send a query. By all means enclose a stamped, self-addressed envelope to make answering easy and to show your professional approach. If you decide to rewrite the newsbreak without querying the editor, enclose a copy of the clipping.

Whether you send a photocopy, the original clipping, or a condensation, always give the source and the date. If someone else submits the item, the earliest date gets the check. Also, select material that won't be quickly dated, as an editor may hold submissions for six months or more.

If you research the information from previously published facts (secondary sources), do send along a bibliography. This protects both you and the editor in the event that some reader locates a source that does not agree with your facts; readers love to point out errors.

The editor may print the clipping exactly or condense it. These items may appear at the end of the page, in a regular column, or as part of a special section such as "Almanac" in *Sports Afield* or "An Encouraging Word" in *Reader's Digest*.

In general, these brief newsbreaks emphasize what goes on in the world today or what went on in the past. They may divulge why we no longer do certain things or why we still do them. These fillers divide logically into oddities and newsbreaks.

FACTUAL ODDITY

The factual oddity may vary in length from a single sentence to several paragraphs, depending on the subject and the market. Try to pack the information into a small capsule of knowledge. Most writers begin with the shorter ones, as they appear frequently in a number of sources. To write even the short ones, you must follow a pattern or formal plan of organization.

1. Patterns In one pattern you compress the facts into one sentence. The first part of the sentence introduces the subject and the rest provides the oddity, as in this excerpt from "Along the Shore," from *Knowledge News Features*.

Fact
In our lifetime our feet will transport us

Expansion
an average of 65,000 miles—or more than 2½ times around the earth.

Some oddities may run to two sentences or more, but in only one paragraph. This one from *Fate*, entitled "Brown Snow Flies in Bulgaria," by W. Ritchie Benedict uses the paragraph style.

Fact

Light brown snow fell in the Razgrad area of Bulgaria in the early spring of 1973, according to a Bulgarian news agency. In some places red hues predominated and accumulation was less than an inch deep.

Expansion

Although colored snow has fallen in the area before, meteorologists have not found an explanation for the phenomenon.

Oddities may include several paragraphs, as does this one from *Fate* for a feature called "Quirks of Fate." It stresses unexplained facts that happen in day-to-day living.

Fact

Since I retired from my office job, . . . I decided to tackle the "catchall" drawer in my . . . desk. . . . I came across one of those pre-printed checks issued as reimbursement for overpayment of seven cents.

Expansion

. . . I put it in my wallet to await an opportunity to cash it.

When the postman arrived about noon . . . my assets increased . . . by $6.70.

Several hours later . . . at the checkout counter in my supermarket I decided to get rid of the two small checks . . . the total due for my groceries—$6.77, the exact total of the two checks.

Outcome

At dinner that evening . . . my husband . . . noticed the date on the grocery slip—June 7, 1967—and pointed out . . . that its briefest numerical representation, 6–7–7, is identical to the cost of the groceries and the total of the two checks—a most unusual three-way coincidence.—DAISY SAYER

If coincidence does not favor you, you can sell a slightly different type of filler to *Fate*. Take a number of related events which happened in different parts of the country and put them together to make a coincidence, as in this example called "How to Sell a Haunted House."

Fact

The weekly newsletter of the Society of Appraisers dated May 10, 1967, published a report on a knotty problem that their members have to face. What is the effect of widespread rumors of ghostly habitation on the value of a house?

Expansion

. . . the general market takes ghosts quite seriously. In some cases a "haunt" depresses the value . . . but it can be used in such a way as to get attention. . . . A realtor and appraiser in Wisconsin . . . advertised "Here is your opportunity to buy a haunted house at a real low cost."

On the other hand a California appraiser cited the case of a property in Oakland which "no one would touch." A man had been murdered in the house and his ghost was rumored to remain there. . . . eventually it sold at 25 percent less than the value of comparable property.

Almost every appraiser has run into the problem of a house that can't seem to hold a tenant. . . . a tenant stayed only one night and explained, "The haunts are too many for me to tackle." . . . The appraiser decided to see for himself. . . . He said, "I found several small trees had grown so that their branches rubbed against a piece of lattice work. Believe me, this was a weird sound. I got a saw and cut off the 'haunts' and the house was never vacant again."

Outcome

One man succinctly summed up realtors' and appraisers' two-way interest in haunts. He observed, "I have not appraised any haunted houses but some of my appraisals have come back to haunt me."

Note that the opening fact and the outcome provide suspense and humor, as well as uniting the diverse events cited in the explanation. All events, however, deal with real estate and "haunts."

2. Markets The subject for an oddity depends on the specialized market. For example, *Fate* or *Beyond Reality* want strange phenomena, but *Knowledge News Features* buys any type of oddity. So you need to actually study the particular magazine in addition to applying the analysis.

A number of markets want historical oddities. Sometimes the question arises as to the definition of "historical." A good rule of thumb would suggest anything that happened twenty-five or more years ago. This oddity by George A. Reynolds from *Military Journal* fits this category.°

Fact

During World War II, Germany produced many phenomena to the imagination. Among them, the jet aircraft, space-conquering rockets, and still more fascinating, the "flying saucer," apparently. The following articles appeared in *The Birmingham News* . . . by war correspondents in the European Theater of Operations. . . .

Expansion

December 13, 1944: "Mysterious Silver Balls Floating in the Air— Pilots (American) report seeing objects, both individually, and in clusters. . . . Their purpose is not immediately evident."

January 2, 1945: A U.S. Fighter base, France, "American fighter pilots engaged in flying night intruder missions over Germany reported the Germans have come up with a new 'secret weapon'—mysterious balls of fire which run along beside their planes for miles. . . . Yank pilots have dubbed them 'foo fighters.' "

Comment

Some pilots have expressed belief that the "foo fighter" was designed strictly as a psychological weapon. . . . it is radio-controlled from the ground, and can keep pace with planes flying 300 miles an hour. . . . there are three types of "foo fighters"—red balls of fire that fly along at wingtip, a vertical row of three balls which fly in front of the planes, and a group of about fifteen lights which follow the planes at a distance, flickering on and off.

Oddities for *Sports Afield*'s "Almanac" need an outdoor angle. Study this one, titled "Knock, Knock."

Fact

A Maine naturalist once trained a pileated woodpecker as a pet. Proud of his wildlife friend, he often let the bird ride on his shoulder like a parrot.

Expansion

This proved to be a mistake however because one day the bird reverted back to nature. In a lighthearted moment it gave its owner a "loving" tap on the side of the head—and knocked him out cold!

A few editors want regional oddities. This historical oddity comes from *The New England Guide*, which requires that particular angle.

Fact

Contrary to a shipload of Indian yarns, movies from silent days, the TV illustrators and hosts of novels, a wooden defensive stockade in early days, per old Ft. No. 4 in Charlestown, was not where the defenders stood, banging away from steaming muskets or Springfields at circling French and Indians.

Expansion

These forts were defended from their log houses, where the shooters were stationed; the stockades kept attackers from setting fire to these houses; posts for these walls were a few inches apart to let the bullets through but no visitors.

Boston Magazine, under the heading "The Reporter," publishes present-day regional oddities. They may discuss unusual items offered for sale by Bloomingdale's or a different image of Bob Eubans (host of "The Newlywed Game") as a competitive rodeo rider and a rock concert promoter.

"The Last Page," from *Car Exchange*, wants oddities about cars and related subjects, such as this one headed "More Visible Then Than Now."

Fact

America's first drive-in service station was opened by the Gulf Refining Company on Dec. 1, 1913, at the intersection of Baum Blvd. and St. Claire in Pittsburgh, Pa.

Expansion

They sold 30 gallons of gas that day at about 6¢ a gallon. Henry Ford Museum, Dearborn, Mich., offers America's first visible pump filling station as part of its Transportation Collection. Built by Raymond Garage Company of Adrian, Mich., in 1915, it operated for 14 years in that city.

These examples should show you the basic structure of the oddity and suggest subjects for special markets. Perhaps you will submit more historical oddities than present-day ones because the research proves easier. Do slant the subject to the magazine and its readers.

NEWSBREAKS

The newsbreak more often deals with fairly current facts. Occasionally, the writer will include some facts from the past to clarify or show motivation. Organize your information around this basic pattern.

1. **Pattern** The pattern may range from a single paragraph to several, depending on the complexity of the subject. It differs slightly from that of the oddity, as shown in this newsbreak from *The Star*.

Fact

Doctors are working on ways to repair damages to the human body—including the brain—with tiny micro-electric "bio-chips."

Expansion

A new "ear" that connects directly to the auditory nerve can already be made by interfacing microelectric systems with living matter, they claim.

"Ideas like this seemed sheer fantasy just a couple of years ago," said Dr. John Barker, who heads a research team at Warwick University in England.

"It will be possible with laser surgery to replace damaged parts of the brain, using bio-chips. Nerve endings grow naturally toward the voltage, and they would just home in on the structure and connect themselves up."

Comment

But Dr. Barker admitted "a mint of money" would be needed to put his theories to work—"maybe as much as the U.S. moon program."

In many of the newsbreaks, you list the source of the information. The one preceding quoted the doctor to give the facts authority. Frequently, the editor (the doctor in the example) adds a comment to make the reader think or chuckle. Let the editor write the comment; you send the facts. In this example from "The Dump Handle," in the *AG-Pilot International*, the editor adds the comment.

Fact

Gypsy Moth in California?. . . That is what we hear.

Expansion

If these pesky little creatures are ever established in that country, there will be hell to pay.

Comment

Wonder what the Sierra Club or hustling environmentalists would say if this happened and no one helped to counter it.

2. Market For *The Star* and *People on Parade* the newsbreak needs only a general appeal to the average reader, but most of the specialty magazines want items that pertain to their readers.

Three of the senior citizen magazines publish columns with newsbreaks, varying in length from 150 to 500 words. Newsbreaks in *Modern Maturity* appear under the title of "Worthy of Note" and cover such subjects as saving energy, recycling, geriatric medicine, coronary deaths, jobs for retirees, revivals of old musicals, or cutting the cost of living.

The *Journal* for the *National Retired Teachers Association* has a comparable section titled "Panorama," but this one gears the news to teachers. Items have included teaching techniques of the future, recycling surplus schools, changing family and lifestyles, fighting crime, protection of health, solar energy, uses of lasers, and even little nostalgic bits on sailing ships, chimney sweepers, and player pianos.

Dynamic Years includes the newsbreaks under "News Worth Filing." The magazine describes the readers as "men and women who are at the height of their careers" and proposes to help them better prepare to live life to the fullest in retirement. The news items discuss such subjects as inflation, legislation, pensions, or anything related to future retirement.

"Notes From All Over" in *Reader's Digest* wants short features, previously published or original, on any subject. The majority appear as reprints but follow the same pattern as this original.†

Fact

Professional golfer Howard Twitty was playing in the 1975 Malaysian Open. His caddie spoke no English, and Twitty couldn't speak the caddie's language.

Expansion

Halfway around the course after Twitty had just taken a club out of his bag, the caddie began to jump up and down, screaming.

Comment

As the confused golfer wondered what on earth the excitement was about, the caddie gingerly turned the golf bag upside down—and out popped a king cobra!—HENRY W. CORAY

In "Time Out for Sports" *Reader's Digest* encourages readers to send in their favorite story from the world of sports only. You may have personally witnessed the action or read about it in a publication. The information may deal with a famous sport figure, such as Johnny Unitas or Althea Gibson, or relate an event that took place in a high school or college setting. To write these, insert dialogue, quotations, and other fictional techniques. Keep the length to under 300 words and cite the source if previously published.

Skydiving asks for material related to that field of interest, as in this example.

Fact

The Uranus Super Skydiving Equipment Company of Bochum, West Germany, is looking to become a European dealer for parachute equipment manufacturers.

Expansion

The company's address is 70 Uterm Scrick, Bochum 00463 West Germany. Eugene Pernak is the contact at that address.

Sports Afield also includes newsbreaks that relate to the outdoors in "Almanac." This one has the title "Ice Havens."

Fact

When the ice got thick enough on Berlin Dam . . . sportsmen witnessed a strange scene.

Expansion

Discarded Christmas trees were dragged out to the frozen lake . . . stacked in piles and bound . . . secured to long stakes . . .

Comes warm weather, the ice will melt. The piles of Christmas trees . . . will sink to the bottom. There they will create underwater havens sought by bass and other varieties of finny creatures in the lake.

Comment

The trees were donated by the nearby community of Canfield, and the Pioneers of America, the service organization for Ma Bell employees. —JOHN KRILL

Women's Sport Magazine buys news about sports, especially about women, for "Sidelines." This short newsbreak on legislation, titled "Pod Bill Killed," appeared in the *Bowhunter Magazine*.

Fact

The Louisiana House of Representatives has killed House Bill 1350

Expansion

which would have allowed the use of drug-tipped arrowheads in certain parishes of the state.

Comment

The vote was 38–57 against the use of the drug succinylocholine chloride by bowhunters.

"I'd advise anyone thinking of submitting material to us," states the editor, "to obtain a copy of the magazine first, as all material must relate to bowhunting. Two examples which come to mind are reports that an Arizona woman recently made history in that state by becoming the first woman bowhunter to tag an Arizona elk and the news from Maryland that a bowhunter there bagged a doe that field dressed at nearly 200 pounds (that's exceptionally heavy for a female deer)."

Montgomery Ward Auto Clubs News wants column material that relates in any way to autos. A very interesting section of newsbreaks appears in *Creative Computing* entitled "Compendium." This section includes any news on the use of computers.

Fact

At Teletronics International's new video center in New York, a computer controls a recently developed system that transfers film images to video tape.

Expansion

The system provides scene-to-scene color correction and has the ability to change and enhance a single color without affecting other colors on the scene. For example, the color of an object, such as a blue soap box, can be corrected without altering flesh tones.

Comment

The computer inserts all the corrections into its memory so that the scene-by-scene changes can be made instantly as the film is transferred to tape.

"An Encouraging Word" in *Reader's Digest* publishes clippings from various sources, but keep the length under 500 words. This reprint from *NBC News* appears typical.§

Fact

Three cheers for

Lockheed Missiles and Space Co. of California, for rescuing a 50,000-volume graduate research collection, soaked when the Stanford University library had a section flood.

§ Copyright © 1979 by The Reader's Digest Association, Inc. Reprinted by permission of NBC News and The Reader's Digest Association.

Expansion

Librarians knew that book covers would mildew long before pages could dry and that they faced a $250,000 loss. But Lockheed volunteered its aid, and the soaked volumes were rapidly trucked to its "Air Space" deep-freeze unit south of San Francisco.

Comment

All moisture was sucked out of the books within the unit. The result: complete restoration.

The reprints in this feature must offer an upbeat ending for a problem in life today.

Mechanix Illustrated buys nonmechanical, short articles of new products of interest to a mechanically inclined readership. This one has the title of "And Now . . . Electric Rickshaw."‖

Fact

We've seen electric vehicles of all kinds come down the pike. Now comes an electric that's *really* different.

Expansion

It's different in that it's not a conversion from gasoline power but rather a conversion from man power. It's the Electric Rickshaw.

. . . this vehicle doesn't look much like the two-wheel cart it's named after.

The Electric Rickshaw, designed by British engineer Roy Haynes, is powered by a dozen 6-volt, 151-amp/hr. batteries that produce a maximum speed of 30 mph. . . .

The rig is 10 ft. long and 5 ft. wide and weighs 1,600 lbs. . . .

Comment

Haynes says that current traction engines are fine. . . .

The Electric Rickshaw is marketed by Haynes Automotive International of Essex, England.

Two photographs accompany this new-product report.

Saturday Review titles its news section "Front Runners," and the length of items may vary from 100 to 1,000 words. The clippings cover such subjects as taping your will, writing like Hemingway, redesigning a McDonald's plastic coffee stirrer, and the Senate.

Fact

Here is a useful note in case you happen to get lost near the Arctic on your next world tour.

Expansion

When Denmark granted Greenland home rule last year, place names were officially changed on the world's largest island. The correct name for Greenland is now Kalaallit Nunaat. When you want the capital, ask the nearest native for Nuuk, not Godthab.

Comment

And God be with you.

"Edubits" in the *Instructor* publishes any type of news that furthers education, as in this example, "Dove," by Kathy Newton.°

Fact

Schools are increasingly recognizing the valuable skills that senior citizens can bring to young people. But how many districts would ask older people to work with special education students?

Expansion

Los Angeles School District does, and the members of the DOVES (Dedicated Older Volunteers in Educational Service), who work with the special-needs children, find the assignment particularly rewarding.

Comment

One DOVE, Arnold Altmark, draws upon 50 years of experience in woodworking to help special-needs kids at East Valley School. "I try to teach my kids a fair amount of self-sufficiency along with the woodworking," he says, "and I think they learn both!"

Newsbreaks for the *Army Reserve* require the military background typical of this one: "Following the Footsteps of Vocational Revolt."

Fact

Army women aren't pigeonholed into secretarial or medical slots. And with the exception of the hard combat skills, more enlisted women are turning up in more places than ever before.

Expansion

In the Army Reserve, about one-third of the 19,000 enlisted women are serving . . . less traditional and non-traditional skills. . . .

In the Active Army, less than half of 50,000 enlisted women are serving in traditional administrative and medical occupations. . . . About 25 percent have shifted toward less traditional skills . . . 30 percent are taking up occupations formerly dominated by men. . . .

A photograph adds to the interest of the newsbreak. Twin photographs showing the Bazooka jeep highlight this news brief from *Military Journal.†*

Fact

These two photos show an interesting field modification to a jeep, manned by T/5 Louis Gergye and Pvt. William Jump of the I & R Platoon, 60th Regiment, 9th Infantry Division.

Expansion

Two 'bazookas' have been mounted on a .50 cal. machine gun pedestal mount; note the two different types of sights and only one retains the foregrip. The hasty construction of sheet steel windscreen and aprons is evident and could not have provided more than limited protection (one can only imagine what it must have been like to drive while looking through that slit!). A third man, the loader, completes the crew—

Comment

certainly a hazardous duty if ever there was one!

"Clippings Cache" in *Lost Treasure* publishes newsbreaks dealing with lost-and-found treasures, metal detecting, and other related subjects. The following newsbreak appeared under the title of "Demolition Treasure."

Fact

Some lucky residents of Cleveland struck it rich recently when workmen began demolishing an abandoned house once owned by the late Albert F. Fletcher.

Expansion

From $80,000 to $100,000 in 50-year-old treasury bills started falling from the walls when the demolition began. Workmen and residents of the neighborhood rushed to gather up the money.

One woman picked up $1,000 and a boy who found a $100 bill hurried off to buy a bicycle.

Comment

Fletcher, who had owned seven houses in Cleveland, died in 1964. Almost $200,000 in savings bonds, cash and gold coins were found in his junk-filled house after he died.

For "Front Entry," *Pillow Talk* wants newsbreaks on matters dealing with romance, marriage, or relationships. "That's Licking the Problem" reports the news this way.

Fact

The latest development in contraceptives—according to a Berlin, New Hampshire, pharmaceutical company—is an edible, glueless stamp coated with a birth-control drug.

Expansion

The stamps are numbered from one to 21, and each day a woman tears off a stamp, moistens it with her tongue, then chews and swallows it.

Comment

Should be a boon to people who have an aversion to pill-taking. Year-long tests are now being conducted on 1,000 female volunteers.

Countrystyle Magazine wants column material and newsbreaks on country-music stars and artists. *Yankee* presents the newsbreaks in "Tintinnabulations," a cartoon feature in which a character comments on the facts. The news must come from the New England area. Read several issues to capture the focus of this unique presentation. *Frets*, a music magazine, needs a guest columnist each month.

These illustrations from a variety of markets should provide enough guidelines to enable you to recognize what sells as oddities and newsbreaks. More important, they should challenge you to find other markets that buy these brief and factual items. While these fillers challenge you to look through the eyes of others, those in the next chapter require viewing your own life with new interest.

*6
Filler Potpourri

These fillers vary widely as to type, pattern, and market, but they offer an easy sale. More important, you need do little research to find them right around you in your home.

RECIPES

Recipes originate in a number of ways. Suppose you have a favorite recipe that all your friends compliment. Or you may have altered a published recipe through your cooking expertise. An old family recipe gets handed down from generation to generation. Regardless of the origin, you want to share it with others.

Editors do not want recipes copied from published cookbooks; they do look for originality. *Do* remember this bit of advice when friends offer you a recipe: By all means find out the source.

1. Long Pattern You may submit the recipe in a long form, using an introductory paragraph. This example from "In the Heart of the Home," *Capper's Weekly*, appeared under the title "Good Things to Eat," by Marian Hansen.

OLD WORLD LEMON SPREAD

Introduction

When jams and jellies are in short supply this time of year, this is a refreshing addition to the menu.

Ingredients

Juice of one lemon
¾ cup water
1 beaten egg
½ cup sugar
1 round tablespoon butter or margarine
1 tablespoon cornstarch
3 drops lemon oil or ½ teaspoon lemon extract

Directions

Combine all ingredients in kettle and stir over low heat until thick. Refrigerate in covered jar. A few grains of salt may be added to bring out the flavor.

"Chefs of the West," a *Sunset Magazine* feature, stresses the art of cooking by men or for men. While the recipe follows the same pattern, the introduction runs longer than the one above and usually gives some historical facts. For example, a recipe on ambrosia told the origin of the dish, then gave the ingredients and the directions for mixing.

"Kitchen Cabinet," in the same magazine, wants a one-sentence introduction suggesting an addition to the recipe before providing the ingredients and the directions.

Outdoor Life asks the reader to send a favorite game or fish recipe. Each month the cooking editor makes other suggestions, such as a recipe for sourdough bread or stuffings for geese and duck and pheasant. The title on this one, "Jim Harding's Tangy Broiled Mollies," emphasizes the masculine slant.

Introduction

This small fish was a unique treat. Mollies (Warmouth Perch) are probably best known in the South, but also are enjoyed in the East, the Great Lakes, and in the West. The meat from this fish is very soft, so don't overcook.

Ingredients

4 whole, cleaned mollies
2 tablespoons lemon juice
¼ cup French dressing
Salt and pepper

Directions

In a bowl, combine lemon juice and French dressing, and marinate fish in it for 1 hour. Remove, salt and pepper, and broil 4 inches from heat for 5 to 8 minutes each side until fish flakes with a fork.
Serves 4.

2. Short Pattern *Women's Circle Home Cooking* wants "Penny Pinchers," as in this example by Naomi Miller called "Next Day's Mashed Potatoes."

Ingredients

10 medium potatoes
1 package (8 oz.) cream cheese
½ pound butter or margarine
1½ cups milk
Paprika

Directions

Boil potatoes after peeling. Add salt. When tender, drain well and mash (preferably with electric mixer) until smooth. Add cream cheese, butter, and scalded milk gradually. Mix until light and fluffy. Put into buttered 2-quart casserole. Cover and refrigerate. Next day, sprinkle with paprika. Bake uncovered for 50 to 60 minutes at 350 degrees.

Countrystyle Magazine wants recipes of country-music stars. *Child Life* prefers healthful recipes, as does *Let's Live*. *Grit*, a national weekly newspaper, publishes recipes, some with holiday features.

In the adult magazines, editors often combine recipes from various people into a column, as *Outdoor Life* and *Sunset Magazine* do. Most major magazines test recipes before they publish them, so make sure what you submit does the job. Although these magazines buy recipes regularly, do search for new markets. If you have any doubt as to whether or not the magazine pays for recipes, write the editor and enclose a self-addressed, stamped envelope.

3. Juvenile Magazines In recent years the juvenile market has shown a growing and continuing interest in recipes that children can handle. *Ebony Jr!* follows the long form of the recipe presentation. As in "Chefs of the West" in *Sunset Magazine*, the opening paragraph focuses on an oddity or historical event. Then it lists the ingredients, necessary equipment, and the directions.

The juvenile magazine *Discovery* publishes a fictional treatment. This abridged example by Elda Bachman gives the recipe for "A Peanut Butter-Jelly Wheatwich."

Introduction

"I'm HUNGRY, Mom."

Hearing these words, a busy mother might say, "Make yourself a snack." So why not learn to make a Peanut Butter-Jelly Wheatwich for yourself and your family or friends? You will need three or four cups of wheat grain . . . sold in health food stores. . . .

Directions

Fill a crock pot two-thirds full with the wheat and cover it with water. Turn the control on low, put the lid on, and let it cook slowly all night. . . . It may be stored in the refrigerator or freezer until needed.

Each time you spread a piece of bread with peanut butter and jelly, take out a tablespoon or more of wheat buds and sprinkle on top. . . .

Comment

Before enjoying your wheat-bud snack made from wheat berries or kernels, thank God for His gift of grain . . . and think of eight-year-old Anna Barkman. According to historical legend, Anna . . . brought the first Turkey Red wheat to central United States from Russia. . . .

Happy munching on your wheatwiches!

Cricket uses a variation of the shorter form, as seen in this example.

FRESH BERRY WHIP

Ingredients

1 cup fresh berries, such as strawberries or blueberries
2 cups milk
½ cup instant nonfat dry milk
¼ cup honey
2 cups (1 pint) vanilla ice cream

Directions

Blender Method

Place the berries in a sieve and rinse under running water. Put all the ingredients, including the berries, into the blender. Make sure the lid is on tightly, then turn on the blender at high speed, slowly count to 20, and turn the blender off.

Electric Mixer Method

Place the ice cream in a dish on the kitchen counter and allow it to soften for about 15 minutes. In the meantime, put the berries in a sieve and rinse under running water. Then transfer the berries to a large mixer bowl and mash them with a fork. Add the milk, dry milk, and honey and blend with the mixer turned on low speed. Then spoon in the ice cream and continue mixing until well blended.

Comment

Berry Whip fills two tall glasses or four small ones.

Other markets using recipes include *Trails, Reflections,* and *Young Judaean.* Since these recipes indicate a new trend in youth magazines—probably because so many mothers work—you may want to check other juvenile markets that buy recipes.

If you hate to cook, then you may enjoy creating brain teasers.

BRAIN TEASERS

To write a brain teaser, you develop your ideas through specific thought patterns, as in the epigram and the quip. Once you master this predetermined way of thinking, you can zip right through creating one of these fillers.

1. **Problem** To write the problem filler, you start with the simple answer and work backward to the beginning. Then you check from the beginning to make sure that the information given leads logically to the answer and that you gave enough hints to move the reader forward, step by step, to the answer. Some editors refer to the problem filler as the "thinker's test." *Grit* published this brief one under the title of "Let's Have Some Fun."

"Two bits a ride!" called the carnival pitchman. Just then two more persons appeared. "Jump on and we'll make it 20 cents each for everyone," he added. Even so, he collected 10 cents more than without the added two. How many took the ride?

Creative Computing wants a much longer problem under the heading of "Puzzles & Problems." Study this abbreviated version.

... Three brothers decided to each chip in $1,000 and buy a car. ... They found the car of their dreams. ... Harry took their $3,000 in cash. When Harry started to enter the transaction into his books he discovered that the price of the car should have been $2,500. Being an honest man Harry called in his assistant, gave him the five $100 bills, and told him to return the money to the brothers. On the way over his assistant decided that since $500 could not be evenly divided among the three brothers he would keep $200 and give each of them back only $100.

... Since each brother ended up by spending only $900, and the assistant kept $200, we get a total of $2,900 accounted for. ... Where did $100 go to?

"Fun Fare," from *Modern Maturity*, publishes the same type of thinker's problems. Sometimes the problem gives five or six clues that describe a famous person, and you try to guess the name by using the least number of hints. Another type of teasers sits five people at a dinner table. From the clues given you try to identify each person at the table.

In the teaser below, *Primary Treasure* asks the reader to find hidden Bible characters in a puzzle devised by Earl Ireland.†

Instructions

Hidden in each one of the sentences below is the name of a Bible man that you will find in the first chapter of Matthew. The first one is given to get you started. See if you can find the others.

1. You will sing a *solo Mon*day morning.
2. Jo rammed her car against a tree.
3. He saw a chimney on the roof.

2. Quiz The quiz appears in many different forms. A very popular one asks the reader to match the numbered items with the lettered facts. In *Primary Treasure* under "Rhyme Time," Linda Kendall asked the reader to match words that rhyme.‡

1.	Sweet	A.	Bent
2.	Breeze	B.	Shell
3.	Neck	C.	Hear
4.	Bed	D.	Wheat
5.	Bee	E.	Ten
6.	Seen	F.	Fed
7.	Deer	G.	Check
8.	Bell	H.	Cheese
9.	Hen	I.	Bean
10.	Cent	J.	Flea

Trails, another juvenile magazine, asks that you match the animal with the right baby, such as *cub* with *bear.*

A number of magazines favor the true-false or straight question-and-answer quiz. "A Capitol Quiz," by J. H. Pollack, appeared in "Post Scripts," *The Saturday Evening Post.*§

Instructions

With the presidential race apparently up for grabs, it is interesting to note that our Chief Executives, like the rest of us, have come in assorted sizes and characters, as the following questions about ten of them show. How many of the ten described can you name?

1. Which President weighed less than 100 pounds?
2. Which President weighed more than 330 pounds?
3. Which President's wife refused to serve liquor or wine in the White House?
4. Which President was taught to read and write by his wife?
5. Which President never saw a map of the United States until he was 19?

Good News, a religious publication, wants the same type of quiz, but with a Christian emphasis. Warren C. Hyam devised this one.

‡ Ibid.
§ Copyright © 1979 by The Saturday Evening Post Company. Reprinted by permission.

Instructions

All of us use phrases or cliches to make a point in conversation.

I wonder if we are aware how many of these phrases come from the Bible? Conversely, some we think are Biblically oriented, are not. In the following quiz you are to separate these phrases. Can you tell which are from the Bible and which are not? Good Luck.

1. I escaped with the skin of my teeth.
2. Cleanliness is next to godliness.
3. All men are liars.
4. We say a red sky at night means a fair day tomorrow.
5. Neither a borrower nor lender be.

The quiz contains fifteen quotations, but this show you the general trend.

A number of quizzes slant to the reader of a specific magazine. For example, "The Last Page" quiz in *Car Exchange* deals with cars or related subjects.

CORVETTE QUIZ

1. What are two styling changes between the 1958 and the 1959 Corvette?
2. What are the external differences between the 1959 and the 1960 Corvette?
3. Corvette was offered as a six or eight cylinder in one year only. What was that year?

This quiz included eight, rather than the usual multiple of five, questions.

A quiz may ask the reader to fill in the blanks. From *New York Antique Almanac* comes this one titled "Remember Radio?" by R. C. McIntyre.

Instructions

Fill the blanks with letters to complete the name or title. The dashes indicate the number of letters needed. The first letter is given to get you off to a good start.

Amos and Andy were listened to by half the nation. The other 50% turned to M _ _ _ and M _ _ _ _ on another station.

Eddie Cantor helped us to grin. His orchestra leader was R _ _ _ _ _ _ _ and his violin.

Another version of "fill in the blanks" resembles a hybrid of acrostics. This one on "American Birds" by Renate Wehje appeared in *Primary Treasure*.‖

```
            A __ __ __ __
            M __ __ __ __ __ __ __ __ __
      __ __ __ E __ __
          __ R __ __ __ __
        __ __ I __ __ __ __ __
  __ __ __ __ __ __ __ C __
          __ A __ __ __ __ __
        __ __ N
            B __ __ __ __ __ __
    __ __ __ __ I __ __ __ __ __
            R __ __ __ __ __
      __ __ __ D __ __ __ __ __
            S __ __ __ __ __ __
```

1. I'm named after a house pet.
2. I can copy other birds' calls.
3. I'm a big bird that likes to live around buildings.

This quiz continues to describe thirteen birds to match the letters of "American Birds." The reader uses the above definitions to name the birds. Under "Let's Discover" this magazine also devises a quiz for each day of the week with answers found in the Bible.

Modern Maturity likewise publishes the completion quiz that emphasizes words. It may list words, for instance, that have the syllable *tain* at the beginning, middle, or end. Anytime you see a quiz in a magazine, check for a by-line; this indicates that the editor buys them. Better still, write and ask the editor what the payment is for quizzes.

3. Puzzles The market for puzzles in both adult and juvenile magazines has greatly increased. The crossword puzzle ranks high in popularity. You can buy the blank crossword puzzle forms and easily train yourself to create them.

Primary Treasure built a puzzle around musical instruments in the Bible. "Daze-A-Head," *Ebony Jr!*, based the words for a puzzle on Christmas presents frequently given. Check several issues of *Young Miss* for puzzles.

The *Church Musician* wants any type of puzzle that highlights music. *Creative Computing* buys word puzzles for "Puzzles & Problems" called "Drop the Letters Puzzles," as in this example.

Instructions

Below is the word *sparkling*. You must drop, or cross out, one letter so that we are left with a new word. You must then cross out another letter which will leave you with yet another new word. You are to continue in this fashion until you have crossed out all but one letter. The last letter should also be a word. At no time can any of the letters be rearranged into a different order to form new words.

Hidden-word puzzles prove equally popular with the adult and the young person. This puzzle by Nancy E. Anderson appeared in *Touch*, under "Hurdles."

Instructions

Listed below are just some of the reasons why we may fail to become friends with certain people. We may feel uneasy about certain characteristics of others and feel hesitant about being friends with them. What type of friend does this make us? Circle each hidden word.

```
L M S O O C R U T C H E S
L I D P N E H Y T U A E B
S L O W L E A R N E R R S
O Y O U N G F T D N I L B
```

crutches   beauty   old   slow learner   young   blind

This partial presentation of the hidden-word puzzle should be sufficient to tell you how to solve it.

Such a puzzle in *Primary Treasure* listed foods that rabbits eat. *Ebony Jr!* chose hidden words that have the sound of *oi* and *oy*.

The adult market publishes more difficult hidden-word puzzles with many more letters. *Modern Maturity* prints one each month, developed around such historical themes as colonial times, boxing's hall of fame, names in uniform. *National Retired Teachers Association Journal* uses a similar monthly puzzle. Previous puzzles centered on the theme of "face the music" or "out of the blue." *World Traveler* listed French words a person might use on tour for its hidden-word puzzle.

You can easily create the hidden-word puzzle. Choose a theme, such as the men who explored the Americas, and compile a list. Place the names from the list on a letter chart as in this example.

```
C  A  R  T  I  E  R              E
O                    L
L                 L
U              A
M           S
B  A  L  B  O  A
U        L
S
```

When you have inserted all names on the chart, fill in other letters of the alphabet.

With a little knowledgeable searching, you can find other types of puzzles that both the adult and juvenile markets buy.

4. Others A number of magazines take riddles like these from *Grit*, titled "Let's Have Some Fun."

What is the fear of lobsters called? Clawstrophobia.

How did the shellfish crash the party? They mussel-ed in.

The juvenile magazines particularly like games that you can develop from props around the house. *R A D A R* showed how to take a box and make an indoor game of marbles. First you cut holes of various sizes in the overturned box; the player tries to roll the marbles through them. The narrower the opening your marble enters, the more points you receive.

Brain teasers and recipes require a certain amount of experimenting, while to sell photo-fillers, you need some know-how with a camera.

PHOTO-FILLERS

With these short fillers the photo may stand alone, or it may supply half the story while your brief caption tells the rest.

1. **Pet Photographs** The confession and pet magazines will buy pictures of your pet. With the picture tell where you found him, name his dominant trait, give a description, relate some antics he has performed—make the reader see him through your eyes. *Do* secure copies from the newsstand and research these markets carefully.

2. **People Photographs** The *National Retired Teachers Association Journal*, under the title of "NRTA Notables," publishes a picture and approximately one hundred words about a retired teacher who has found ways to use his or her skills to help others. For example, a retired teacher may substitute in schools, start a nursery school, or become a writer. First introduce the personality and tell what he or she taught, then relate what he or she now does. *Modern Maturity* in "Spotlight on People" buys the same type of picture and text, except that the personality may have retired from any profession. Since *Dynamic Years* only *prepares* the reader for retirement, "Dynamic Americans" uses color photographs and descriptions of preretirees doing a great job. Most of these magazines you can obtain only by subscription, but how better to invest your money?

"Looking at People," in *Runner's World*, stresses information on joggers. You may send either a black-and-white or color picture of the person. "Former Champ Palomino Stays Sharp" comes from "Looking at People."

Background

Carlos Palomino, 50, is unique among boxers. The only man to score the unique "double" of capturing the world championship and a college degree simultaneously, Palomino is also one of the few fighters to continue running after retiring from the ring.

Today

"At the end of my career it became very hard to do the running day after day. But when I retired, I began to really enjoy getting up and jogging five, six, sometimes ten miles."

Palomino, now an actor, recently appeared in *Marciano*.

Most of the short picture-profiles in the other magazines follow this example but slant to their readers for strong identification.

Ebony, in "Speaking of People," features a photograph of an outstanding black person. A short biography accompanies it, telling about his background, including facts about his family, education, and any other information to show why he merits this recognition.

One confession market wants a picture of your child and fifty words about what endears him or her to you. *Small World* in "Small Talk" buys color pictures and information about how owners use their Volkswagens. A recent issue depicted a police department, an owner of a hunting dog, and a man with a large family, all adapting the VW to specialized use.

3. Photograph Only Under "Flip Shots," *Golf Magazine* takes pictures of celebrity golfers with emphasis on the hairstyle. One photograph showed a windblown look for Dave Hill and a "natural" for Tom Weiskopf. Almost any person can snap these unposed shots.

Candid shots of babies or tots are popular with a few magazines. Send the photograph and let the editor write the caption.

For the "Photo Finish" section, *Sport Magazine* does not want an actual picture but rather a description of a particular situation involving a sports figure. In making your nomination you want to give the *who, when, where, what,* and *why* of the action. The magazine will shoot the picture. Read the magazine for a lead about the copy. The published pictures should give you the slant.

So keep your camera handy to take a picture of a pet, outstanding person, sports figure, or child. Don't toss out the funny photos of your children; share them—and use the money you receive to start the children's bank accounts.

ONE OF A KIND

These fillers have only one specialized market.

1. **Redbook** Redbook buys original baby announcements. The parents must submit the original announcement within six months of the date of birth or of adoption. In the case of an adopted-child announcement, the magazine restricts the baby's age to not more than a year old. The announcement must originate with the parents and must have actually been used to announce the date of birth or adoption.

To give you an idea of the kind previously submitted, parents by the name of Mingo used a facsimile of a bingo card to announce the date of birth and the baby's weight, with the child's name in the center. In another, the father, an architect, drew specifications for a house addition, then gave the pertinent facts about the baby. Photographer parents announced a recent development, giving the vital facts in photographic jargon, such as "good color," "well-composed," "sharp," and "continuing development."

In short, the announcement should cleverly highlight the backgrounds of the parents—hobby, business, or whatnot—along with the vital statistics of the baby.

2. **Weekly Newspapers** The editor's note in the *National Enquirer* reads: "When you spot a goof on TV, write us about it, being sure to include the name of the show, network, and date of the telecast." One such filler told how a private eye in a television series buttoned up his shirt, but the next picture showed the shirt completely open.

Grit and a few others will buy a short pet peeve. Try to state the peeve in one sentence, as in this example from *Grit*.

> My pet peeve is being tail-gated by an impatient speeder trying to pass me on a two-lane highway when I am trying to stick to the 55 mph speed limit.—TINA SIMS

National Enquirer wants pictures of unusual signs, usually along the highway. One sign said: "Caution: Aircraft Have Right of Way on Road." The photograph must tell a story without needing words for explanation, but it can depict any subject matter whatever. A brief note should accompany the photograph, giving the location of the sign and the reason for it.

No text can completely cover all types of potpourri fillers, but this discussion should inspire you to search for other specialized markets.

If you find specialization too much trouble, then consider a more general filler, the joke.

7*
Laughter

Someone once described laughter as God smiling on a troubled world. An amusing filler gives everyone a good laugh, and few people care whether the incident really happened and received some editing, or whether the writer contrived it out of "whole cloth." Regardless of its origin, the joke has only one purpose—to evoke laughter.

PATTERNS

The joke or laughing matter may appear on a special humor page, such as "Light Housekeeping" in *Good Housekeeping* or "Parting Shots" in *American Legion Magazine*. These humorous bits also frequently complete a page in a magazine. Regardless of the placement, the joke develops around a number of different patterns.

1. Dialogue Pattern This pattern eliminates any trimmings and merely relates exactly what each person says, as in a stage play. Tag the speakers by profession, name, sex, or the like. The character projection may or may not contribute to the humor.

The first person speaking states the situation. The second one plays the straight man or asks the question. Then the first speaker delivers the punch line, reversal, or put-down. Frank C. Mathews wrote this example for "Family Sense and Nonsense" in *Today's Christian Parent.*°

°Copyright © 1980 by Standard Publishing. Reprinted by permission of the author and the publisher.

MAID: I'm sorry. Mrs. Black said to tell you she is not at home.
VISITOR: That's all right. Just tell her I'm glad I didn't come.

You'll find almost the same pattern, but more compressed, in "Fun Factory," *Career World*.

SHOPPER: Holy cow! Beef is higher than ever!
SHOPKEEPER: No, it isn't. . . . It was higher when the cow jumped over the moon.

In the joke one person may do the only speaking, as in this one from "Grins and Chuckles," in *Grit*.

The violinist at a private musicale was playing a difficult concerto that contained some particularly long rests for the soloist. During one of these intervals, a kindly old woman leaned toward the performer and whispered loudly:
"Why don't you play something you know, my boy?"

A joke may set the scene and then let the characters talk. *Humorama, Inc.* provides this excerpt.†

The father was trying to fix a door that didn't hang right.
"Hey, son," he called to his teen-age youngster, "get me a screwdriver, will you please?"
Just as the father was getting impatient, the youth finally appeared.
"Gee, Dad," he said apologetically, "I've got the orange juice but I can't find the vodka!"

"The Funny Side," *Midnight/Globe*, lets the two characters develop the joke.

The patient burst out, "Doctor, you should be ashamed to charge so much for office calls! You live in a mansion and ride in a limousine, all at your patients' expense!"
"Why, shame on you," the doctor reprimanded him. "I was just going to name my yacht after you."

†Copyright © 1980 by Humorama, Inc. Reprinted by permission.

2. Compressed Pattern You can deliver the joke in a declarative sentence, or a question, as in this joke from "Grins and Chuckles," in *Grit*.

> A lawyer declared to an all-male jury: "Gentlemen, shall this charming young lady be cast in a lonely cell, or shall she return to her beautiful little apartment at 34 Wilson Avenue, telephone 8–7765?"

Some jokes even eliminate the speaker and talk directly to the reader: "Did you hear about the man who cut his wisdom teeth by biting off more than he could chew?"

This joke, from "Dear Suzie," *Midnight/Globe*, uses a sign to compress the humor.

> This dressmaker's ad proves the English language is wonderful: "Bring your ill-fitting problems to this old sew-and-sew."—MIKE HALLEY

A joke may imply the existence of other characters. Study this example from "Grins and Chuckles," in *Grit*.

> The preacher said: "Brothers and sisters, my sermon this morning will be about liars. Now, has everyone read the 30th chapter of Matthew?"
>
> Half the hands in the congregation went up.
>
> "You're just the people I want to talk to," said the preacher. "There is no such chapter."

Other brief forms of the joke rely on such introductions as "Overheard at a particular place." Notice how the lead-in contributes to the humor in this illustration.

> Overheard at a fund-raising committee: "Today we do a lot more begging on expensive letterheads than with tin cups."

Sometimes you merely give a person-to-person introduction, as in this joke.

One woman to another: "It's not hard to diet these days; just eat what you can afford."

The preceding examples show you various ways to compress the joke but still get a laugh. Some material, however, requires the full pattern for a chuckle.

3. Long Pattern In the long pattern, the first paragraph shows the problem situation, introduces the characters in conflict, and hints at the ending. At times, setting plays an important part. Let's analyze this joke from "The Funny Side," in *Midnight/Globe*.

Situation

A man having trouble with termites under his porch finally asked the aid of a professional exterminator.

In a line of dialogue you let the expert ask a question that gives the owner an opportunity to quip.

Complication

"What have you tried so far?" asked the expert.

The last speech lets the sympathetic character deliver the punch line.

Punch Line

"I tried poking at them," said the man. "But every time I do, they chew the end off the stick!"—JACK R. KISER

Humorama, Inc. makes a slight variation in the complication with several lines of dialogue. ‡

Situation

A woman, having an upstairs room of her house painted, thought the painter was making slow progress. She couldn't hear a sound.

‡ Copyright © 1967 by Humorama, Inc. Reprinted by permission.

Complication

"Painter," she called, "are you working?"
"Yes, ma'am," came the reply.
"I can't hear you," the woman said.

Punch Line

"Well," the painter called down to her, "I'm not putting it on with a hammer!"

In this one from "Parting Shots," *American Legion Magazine,* the situation also summarizes some of the action.§

Situation

A cowboy with nothing much to do ambled into a blacksmith's shop and picked up a horseshoe without realizing it had just come from the forge. Instantly, he dropped it, shoved his seared hand into his pocket and tried to act nonchalant.

Complication

"Kinda hot, wasn't it?" chided the blacksmith.

Punch Line

"Nope," replied the cowpoke, "just don't take me long to look at a horseshoe."—JOHNIE WILSON

This joke, entitled "A Taste of Authority," comes from "Post Scripts" in *The Saturday Evening Post.*‖

Situation

At a company-sponsored first aid course, the instructor singled out one of the workers. "What is the first thing you would do if you discovered you had rabies?"

Complication

"I'd locate my supervisor," the man replied.
"Then what would you do?" the instructor asked.

Punch Line

"Bite him," the man replied.—LANE OLINGHOUSE

Playboy, under the feature "Party Jokes," uses any of the patterns as does *Reader's Digest* for "Laughter, the Best Medicine."

Humor does not develop as spontaneously as it appears to on delivery; a lot of work goes into getting laughs. Choose a strong reader-identification situation and find a good punch line that will fit it. Then work backward, choosing the characters and the necessary dialogue. This approach to writing a joke also works very well with children's humor.

CHILDREN'S HUMOR

The bright sayings of children have a large market because of the wide reader identification; look in any direction and you will find either parents or grandparents repeating such humorous stories. The limited knowledge of children and their application of what they do know often combine to produce laughter. Following a pattern will help in projecting this kind of humor.

1. Choosing a Pattern Some patterns differ slightly from the adult joke. In one pattern, you summarize the situation and then let the child deliver the punch line, as in this example from *Grit*, in "Bright Sayings."

Situation

When my wife and I were discussing longevity, I made the remark that how long a person lived depended a lot on his genes.

Complication and Punch Line

Our five-year-old son, listening to every word, suddenly exclaimed, "Dad, I just hope when I get old I'm wearing the right pants!"—W. E. JOHNSON

Sometimes you combine the situation and the complication. Note this combination from *Good Housekeeping.*†

†Copyright © 1967 by The Hearst Corporation. Reprinted by permission.

Situation and Complication

"See that cat?" I boasted to my four-year-old. "I changed him from a sick, skinny kitten to the big, beautiful, healthy cat he is now."

Punch Line

Bess was fascinated. "Are you a witch?" she asked. —ROLLIE HOCHSTEIN

Mostly, you write this filler using the full form or all three steps: situation, complication, and punch line. This example appeared in "Bright Talk" in *Dixie Roto*, titled "Alien World."

Situation

Bonnie Sue, my five-year-old granddaughter, was visiting us from New Orleans.

The first night with us, she cried after I put her to bed.

Complication

"What's the matter, Bonnie Sue?" I asked.

Punch Line

"I can't sleep," she replied. "Because it's not my own dark, and I can't hear Daddy playing the stereo."—ELIZE BRENNEN

The pattern you choose depends on which one the market uses most frequently and which one will show your material to the best advantage. You will see the full pattern in most cases.

2. Projecting the Humor Certain combinations of circumstances produce the humor. In this example from *American Baby*, "Chuckles and Cherubs," the humor develops from the wrong associations.

Situation

While out to lunch with my sister and her four-year-old son, Davey, my nephew decided he wanted a bowl of soup and asked his mother to read the choices available. When she got to chicken gumbo, Davey said excitedly, "That's the kind I want."

Complication

He could hardly wait for the waitress to serve him, and my sister was confused because he had never had that kind of soup before.

Punch Line

When the soup arrived, a cloud of disappointment came over his face as he spooned through the soup. Finally he looked up and exclaimed, "But, Mom, where are the gumballs?"

The child's description of the situation can produce the humor, as in "Dog-gone," from "Things Kids Say" in *The Star.*

Situation

My four-year-old granddaughter, Christina, was sitting on the floor eating an ice cream cone. Missy, her new puppy, jumped into her lap and started eating off the cone. Christina started to cry and wouldn't eat the cone.

Complication and Punch Line

I said: "Chris, eat your cone," and she replied: "I can't, Nana, it has dog lips all over it."—RUTH BOEHME

Occasionally, the child applies what he knows to the situation, as in "Feels Sick about It," in *Capper's Weekly.*

Situation and Complication

My pregnant sister's four-year-old son was getting a sound talking-to for being naughty during the day. His dad said, "I was telling the guys at the office today about what a good boy you are and then I come home to this! How do you think this makes me feel?"

Punch Line

My nephew replied, "I don't know about you, Dad, but it makes me feel pregnant!"

All of the previous examples used minor-character viewpoint, in that a mother, grandmother, uncle, or other relative reported on the major character, a child. This filler from "Post Scripts" in *The Sat-*

urday Evening Post, titled "Food for Thought," repeats a similar situation of the wrong application.°

Situation

"Mommy, my tummy aches," complained little Sally.

"Never mind, dear," comforted her mother. "It's only because it's empty. It will feel better when you get something in it."

Complication

At the weekly bridge session that afternoon, one of the ladies mentioned she had a headache.

Punch Line

"You'll feel better after you get something in it," she said.—SAMUEL J. STANNARD

Note that this example and the next one use implied viewpoint to relate the incident. Children often create humor when they transfer rules laid down for them to a different situation. *Catholic Digest* provided this selection.

Situation

On a train a woman sat beside a little girl who was holding a doll in her lap.

Complication

The woman asked cheerily, "Does your dolly talk?"

Punch Line

"Yes," replied the child politely. "But not to strangers."—C. KENNEY

The humorous situation can result when a child imitates in the wrong place something he or she has seen done at home. "In Our Parish" in *Catholic Digest* published this one.

Situation

In our parish in Bloomington, Minnesota, four-year-old Lisa had learned a new game.

Complication

As the surprised usher waited with his collection basket, she removed a nickel from her clenched little fist, spun it in the air, and shouted, "Heads!"

Punch Line

She caught it, studied it, frowned, then calmly dropped it into the basket.—MRS. J. B. BUTTS

Children appear funniest when they truthfully sum up a situation, as in this illustration from "Laughter, the Best Medicine," in *Reader's Digest*.†

Situation

Asked about the first day of school,

Complication

a kindergartner offered his considered judgment:

Punch Line

"I learned a lot of stuff there, but it sure cuts into my day."

Laughter can develop when a child mispronounces a word or misunderstands what he or she hears. This filler, "Cafeteria Memory," appeared in "Bright Talk," *Dixie Roto*.

Situation

At dinner recently, we were discussing food we especially like.

During the conversation, the children startled me by informing us they liked the vegetables the school cafeteria served better than they liked mine.

Complication

Then Greg, 11, added to my confusion by interjecting, "You know what? I really like that fruit amnesia they serve."

Punch Line

It took me a minute or two to know he meant ambrosia.—ALMA E. HEMELT

In truly describing a situation, the youngster can give the wrong impression. This example comes from "Chuckles from Cherubs," in *American Baby.*

Situation

I was trying to get the catsup out of the bottle to put the finishing touch on my son Walter's sandwich.

Complication

Just then the doorbell rang and Walter went to answer it.
"Is your Mom home?" the caller asked.

Punch Line

"Yeah," Walter replied. "She's out in the kitchen hitting the bottle."—MRS. G. G. CRABTREE, from Walter Crabtree

This market wants the name of the child so as to make the payment to the youngster who created the humor.

The unexpected logic children display will furnish a chuckle. "Things Kids Say" from *The Star* titles this one "Walking Tall."

Situation

After hearing everyone telling my three-year-old daughter how big she was on her birthday, my six-year-old son was feeling rejected.

Complication and Punch Line

Standing up he asked us to look and proudly said: "I'm big, too. Look at me. I go all the way from the floor up."—LINDA DAVIS

The evasive child may follow the spoken instructions—but only up to a point. *Parish Family Digest* published this example. ‡

---

‡ Copyright © 1967 by Our Sunday Visitor. Reprinted by permission.

Situation

When I looked out the window to see what my small son was doing, I saw him by the garage. He was covered with mud from head to toe. I went out and marched him straight to the bathroom. "Get out of those clothes and get in the bathtub," I ordered.

Complication

Later when I went to wash him, I found him sitting there playing with his tub toys. The tub had no water in it. "How come there's no water in the tub?" I asked.

Punch Line

"You never told me to put any water in the tub," he answered.
—MARGIE BUSHONG

Sometimes the child goes beyond obeying the order of the parent, as in this selection from "Chuckles from Cherubs," *American Baby*.

Situation

I had difficulty getting my four-year-old daughter to brush her teeth. One evening after finally coaxing her to brush her teeth after dinner she spent almost twenty minutes in the bathroom.

Complication

I went to check on her and find out what was taking her so long.

Punch Line

She turned to me and said, "I brushed my teeth three times so I won't have to do them tomorrow."—MRS I. MARKEY, from Debbie Markey

Another humorous situation involves the correct use of a word applied to the wrong situation. This selection appeared in "Laughter, the Best Medicine" in *Reader's Digest*.§

Situation and Complication

Returning from her first day at school, a youngster was asked by her mother if she had been assigned a new teacher for the ensuing year.

§ Copyright © 1966 by The Reader's Digest Association, Inc. Reprinted by permission.

Punch Line

She hesitated before replying, "I don't believe so—I think she's used."—ALPHA EGER

Sometimes you can compress the humor, as does this example from "Dear Suzie" in *Midnight/Globe*.

Situation and Complication

My five-year-old asked if she could call me by my first name. "Why should I have to call you Mommy," she said,

Punch Line

"you don't call me child."—DIANE BLAKLY

The child with a one-track mind gets a laugh in this excerpt from *Parish Family Digest*, called "I Am Going to Be a Sister."‖

Situation

In our parish school one little girl exclaimed that she was going to be a sister when she grew up.

Complication and Punch Line

Her friend quickly responded to her intention, saying, "Renee, you can't be a sister because you don't have a brother."—SISTER ROBERTA ANN LESKEY, CSB/Philadelphia

To write "from-the-mouths-of-babes," begin with what the child said. Then create the situation that led to this remark. The complication must puzzle the reader and lead to the punch line.

Jokes and children's humor bring laughter to a troubled world. So tune in on the conversations of others and see if you can do your part to share a few chuckles.

Anecdotes offer still another way to bring cheer to a dull day.

*8
Anecdotes

The anecdote as a reflection of the American way of life briefly reports true incidents and happenings. Most of these anecdotes amuse the reader, but a few have a serious tone.

Viewpoint in the anecdote depends upon your role as the writer. If the action centers on you, then write from first-person major-character viewpoint. When another character dominates the action but you relate it, choose first-person minor-character viewpoint. In some anecdotes you merely report the action, unidentified, with implied viewpoint. Your material and the pattern will help you choose the best viewpoint.

PATTERNS

In an anecdote one person becomes the aggressor, while the other one has the reader's sympathy. As in the joke or children's humor, the outcome of the anecdote varies from a humorous reversal to a put-down. The characters offer the key to the outcome and frequently to the specific pattern.

Choose one of two patterns to develop the anecdote. You may write the anecdote as a scene similar to that of the joke, or as a "slice of life." In the *scene* the reader becomes involved in the action with the first-person major- or minor-character viewpoint. For the *slice-of-life*, the reader merely observes the action as reported by another—with or without identification.

1. **Scene** As in the joke, the first paragraph of the anecdote describes the situation and involves two characters in action. Tags

quickly project the characters to the reader with a minimum of words and show them in conflict. The opening paragraph tells where and generally when the action takes place. Most important, give a hint to the ending so you do not shock the reader or create an anticlimax. "Laughter, the Best Medicine," in *Reader's Digest* provides this illustration for analysis.°

Situation

Leo Durocher was coaching at first base in an exhibition game the Giants played at West Point. One cadet sitting in the stands was trying his best to ride Leo.

This paragraph introduces the two characters in conflict, tagging them by background or occupation. It sets the time and place, and implies the ending through the words, *West Point* and *cadet*.

Complication

"Hey, Durocher!" the West Pointer yelled. "How did a little squirt like you get into the major leagues?"

This second paragraph develops the conflict.

Outcome

Leo's one-line reply left the cadet cheering-section in stiff silence. "My Congressman appointed me," he said.

This third paragraph delivers the squelch that catches the heckler off guard.

2. Slice-of-Life Usually, the writer acts as the observer and merely narrates what happens. Set the scene by telling when the action takes place, and name the characters involved, as in this filler from "Life in These United States," *Reader's Digest.*†

Situation

At dividend time in the Savings and Loan Association, one elderly woman was finding it wearisome to remain on her feet as the line moved slowly toward the window. She took off her shoes, left them in her place in line and went over to sit in a comfortable chair in the lobby.

This paragraph introduces the character along with the time and place but offers no conflict.

Complication

The others in line cooperated, pushing her shoes along as the line moved, until

Outcome

the woman regained her place, calmly stepping into her shoes just as they reached the window.—MARSHALL GILLER

This type of anecdote demands more writing skill, as the action must speak for itself and move the story forward. You must not overwrite or overplay the action, or the reader will not believe the anecdote really happened. If anything, you need to underplay the action, and let the reader's imagination help him or her visualize what happened.

This anecdote from "Life in These United States" combines the two patterns effectively.‡

Situation

My husband took our dog to the veterinarian and sat in the waiting room with the other dog owners. Suddenly the street door opened a few inches and an authoritative voice called, "Better get a tight hold on your animals!"

Complication

Everyone grasped his pet protectively, nervously wondering what sort of brute was to be led in.

‡ Ibid.

Outcome

The door opened slowly—and in walked the mailman. He dropped some letters on a table, grinned, and walked out.—MRS. ROY J. OLSON

This anecdote adds dialogue, characterization, and emotional reaction to the slice-of-life pattern. The final line provides the reversal.

To determine the best pattern for your material, write the anecdote both ways or try a combination. Choose the one which most effectively projects the humorous action. As a final check, analyze your chosen market for the pattern that appears most frequently. Only you can make this final decision.

MARKETS

In the last decade magazines have changed from general to specialty, as previously mentioned, so the anecdote reflects this specialization. While magazines do buy general anecdotes with any type of background, the specialized markets restrict the backgrounds to their readers' interest. Although *Reader's Digest* has a number of features that require specific backgrounds—college, the military, Americana, or business—it also buys general anecdotes. On the other hand, *Runner's World* wants anecdotes that deal only with runners.

1. **General Anecdote** The general anecdote relies on a reader-identification situation and familiar characters, but no specific background. The "Letters" section of *The Star* published this general anecdote.

Situation

I was very tired and almost going to sleep watching television.

Complication

My husband was very quiet, too, until he turned to me during a commercial and said:

Outcome

"What happened to our marriage? We used to talk during the commercial breaks."—JANICE FISCHER

Reader's Digest uses the general anecdote at the end of a page.§

Situation

One of our friends composes modern music—the blunt and angry kind. His grandmother, who adores him, is not so adoring of his music, preferring the harmonies of Mozart and Beethoven.

Complication

After her grandson's first concert, the young composer joined his grandmother, the applause still ringing in his ears. "Well, how did you like it?" he inquired happily.

Outcome

"My boy," she said, "if this was in your head, I'm glad it came out."—DAGMAR V. SMID

Reader's Digest also reprints anecdotes from other magazines. Frequently, *Reader's Digest* will notify you that it will hold your anecdote, but gives you permission to submit it elsewhere. The editor requests that if you sell it you send along the name of the publisher for reprint identification. So you collect two payments for the same anecdote. If you don't sell it elsewhere, it may still appear in *Reader's Digest*.

Catholic Digest also offers a good market for the general anecdote. The anecdote may follow either pattern or a combination.

Situation

A summer vacationist was visiting the Smokies for the first time. She spent all of her first day horseback riding along one of the many trails high in the mountains.

Complication

She was so impressed by the beauty of the scene she beheld that when she returned to the riding stable she turned to the old gentleman who

§Ibid.

rented the horses and remarked haughtily, "I don't suppose you natives have any idea of what a wonderful view you have here!"

Outcome

"We appreciate it enough to live here all year 'round, lady," the old gentleman replied.—JIM HEWITT

2. Religious Anecdote *Catholic Digest* buys religious-background anecdotes for "In Our Parish," discussed in the previous chapter. While many of these deal with children, some focus on adults. This one appeared at the end of the page.

Situation

Father Joseph Kearney offered the invocation at a luncheon meeting of the National Maritime Union. He also spoke a few words on labor-management relations.

Complication

"I don't know whether to cheer or applaud," one listener told another. "But what can you say after a prayer?"

Outcome

"As I recall, it's always been OK to say 'Amen,'" replied the other.—WARREN A. MCGOWAN

Christian Adventurer used this anecdote with the title of "$25 Answer."

Situation

An earnest Christian woman was engaged in her ministry to doctors, nurses, and patients in a hospital.

Complication

A doctor facetiously said to her, "Do you believe God will hear your prayer? I'm hard up. If I asked Him, would He send me $25?"

The good woman answered, "If you were introduced to the President, would you put your hand in his pocket at once?"

"No," he said, "not until I knew him better."

Outcome

"You need to be a great deal better acquainted with God before you can expect such an answer as you wish."

Do not equate an anecdote with a minister/priest character with a religious anecdote. Note, in the preceding examples, that each brought out a religious principle.

3. Americana Anecdote A number of magazines emphasize the American way of life. In writing for "Life in These United States" in *Reader's Digest*, try to name the specific state, emphasize character tags typical of the area, and give action that dominates the district. Consider this example.‖

Situation

A West Virginian worked at a factory in a neighboring state. Telling his co-workers about a forthcoming trip back to his native state, he said, "Martha and me are repairin' to go on a little vacation back to West Virginny."

Complication

A fellow worker interrupted, "You mean you're preparing to go on a trip, not repairing. To repair means to fix something."

Outcome

"That's what I said," retorted the mountaineer. "We're fixin' to go."—JACK LAND

Most readers associate the art of quilting with early Americans. This anecdote by Caryl Hansen appeared in *Quilt World*.¶

Situation

The scrunch of gravel outside the guest room next to our bedroom alerted me. Half-dressed, I jumped out of view, hiding from whoever was walking past our bedroom window, and I heard the door to the meter box open. Only the meter reader from the utilities company,

‖Ibid.
¶From November/December 1979 issue. Reprinted by permission of the House of White Birches, Inc., Seabrook, N.H.

and I relaxed. He'd nearly caught me overexposed on previous early morning visits.

Complication

I heard the box slam and the footsteps retreat. Then, abruptly, they stopped. I waited for the sound of gravel or the bang of the front gate. Nothing. At last I pulled on jeans and sweater and peeked cautiously out our bedroom window. No one in sight. I tiptoed down the hall and flung open the guest room door.

A friendly but unfamiliar face, pressed against the guest room window, smiled in at me.

"I'm admiring your quilt," the new meter reader shouted through the glass, pointing at the bed. "Is it old?"

I nodded, then shouted back, "It belonged to my great-aunt."

"I thought so. Nine-square, but very unusual with that border around each block. Hope you don't mind my stopping to look. I collect quilts."

Outcome

With that, the meter reader gave me a cheery wave. "Well, thanks," she called, and I watched, smiling, as she disappeared around the corner of the house, banging the gate behind her.

Maine must always provide the background for *Down East* anecdotes. This one, entitled "Pronounced Flavor," comes from "It Happened Down East."

Situation

A friend of mine from Oregon, who is especially fond of seafood, recently spent a week in Bar Harbor at the home of my cousin. No one who heard my cousin talk would believe he came from anywhere else other than the State of Maine.

Complication

Before my friend returned home, she asked her host once more the name of the delicious fish served for supper the night before. "Swordfish," he replied.

Outcome

A few weeks later he received the following note: "I've been trying to find that wonderful fish out here, but nobody seems to have heard of sodfish."—ELIZABETH YOUNG

4. College Anecdote *Reader's Digest* features a section on "Campus Comedy." In this type of filler, you make the setting a college campus and develop the humorous action of the characters in this environment. While the anecdote may use any pattern, this one combines the complication and the outcome.°

Situation

A mother asked a dean of admissions if her son's excellence on the rock-'n-roll guitar would carry any weight in getting him into college.

Complication and Outcome

"Five years ago, maybe yes," wrote the admissions man. "But now we are looking for some listeners."—DAVID LIPSKY, quoted by Robert Sylvester in *Chicago Tribune–New York News Syndicate*

5. Sport Anecdote Two golf magazines want true anecdotes relating to unforgettable golf experiences. In "Only in Golf" from *Golf* comes this slice-of-life anecdote.

Situation

On a visit to Los Angeles, my son and I played golf at Griffith Park with a young woman who used tees in the fairways. About the middle of the third hole she borrowed a few yellow tees from us.

Complication

"I've plenty of red tees," she said. "But those are used in the rough, aren't they?"

Outcome

We explained that we were strangers and did not know the rules of the club.—MITCH SENA

This anecdote from "Rub of the Grin," *Golf Digest*, follows the scene pattern, but the magazine takes any pattern.

Situation

The famous course at St. Andrews, Scotland, has one bunker known as "Hell," because it's so hard to get out of.

°Copyright © 1966 by The Reader's Digest Association, Inc. Reprinted by permission.

A visiting American clergyman had been warned about this trap, but landed in it anyhow. He took his niblick and made a perfect shot, landing the ball on the green.

Complication

Turning proudly to the caddie, he said, "And what do you think of that?"

Outcome

"I think when ye die, ye'd better take yer niblick with ye."
—B. HUFF

From *Sports Afield* "Almanac" comes this anecdote in the slice-of-life pattern.

Situation

An ingenious teacher new to Grangeville, Idaho, and unfamiliar with the fishing potential and hot spots of her new area, hit on a novel solution to the problem.

Complication

Assigning her 35 students a 200-word theme entitled, "My Three Favorite Fishing Holes," she got the inside dope on over 50 spots.

The assignment required the students to list the best lures or baits, the selections of the streams or lakes which were best, the species and sizes of fish, and the best roads or trails to take.

Outcome

Within a week, she had learned about areas that even old-timers weren't aware of. She gave 35 A's!

Runner's World chose this anecdote for publication.

Situation

At the ill-fated (President Carter dropped out halfway) Catoctin 10-kilometer race near Camp David, a race within the race was occurring. Spurred by the running habits of the President, the three security branches of the government have found it necessary to include experienced runners along with the usual agents.

Complication

Though necessarily anonymous, the FBI, Secret Service and CIA ran their own competition. The results: the FBI came in first, the CIA placed second and the Secret Service brought up the rear.

Outcome

Later, and in the spirit of fair play, Carter explained the outcome wasn't really a true test because, "The Secret Service had to follow me."

6. Military Anecdote Along with *Reader's Digest* a number of military-oriented magazines buy anecdotes with this type of background. *Army Magazine* published this slice-of-life anecdote.†

Situation

During the big Washington, D.C., winter snow storm last year, a local radio station announced school closings, road conditions, cancellations of meetings and postponements of special events.

Complication

The announcer relayed the message that liberal leave policy for government personnel was in effect and that only essential people should report for duty at the Pentagon.

Outcome

Later in the day, the same broadcaster laughingly reported that the entire Pentagon work force showed up.—COL. GLENN E. FANT, AUS, retired

The slice-of-life anecdote runs much shorter than the scene one, but this market buys both types equally.

"Humor in Uniform" in *Reader's Digest* does not restrict the anecdote to servicemen only; instead it may give a sidelight on the military family.‡

† From January 1980 issue. Copyright © 1980 by The Association of the U.S. Army. Reprinted by permission.

‡ Copyright © 1966 by The Reader's Digest Association, Inc. Reprinted by permission.

Situation

One day when our little girl was in that intermediate stage when she wore a diaper only at night, I went out for an evening of bridge, leaving my husband to put her to bed.

Complication

Later it occurred to me that he wouldn't know where to find the diaper pins. I needn't have worried.

Outcome

When I arrived home I found the child peacefully asleep. Her diaper was secured on one side with a major's leaf. On the other side was an artillery insignia. At the front of the diaper my husband had hopefully pinned a Good Conduct ribbon.—WILMA SHEARD

United States Naval Institute accepts only true and never previously published accounts of humorous happenings. This illustration meets that requirement.

Situation

During a captain's mast on board the newly commissioned USS *Texas* (CGN-39), a young sailor was before the CO due to an unauthorized absence. In his defense, his division officer and his peers spoke highly of his performance.

Complication

The captain asked the accused how he could be such a good sailor in his division officer's eyes yet goof up and be absent for several days without permission.

Outcome

Without a moment's hesitation, the young sailor replied, "Well, Sir, I'm flexible."—LT. (junior grade) ERNEST N. HAYDEN, USN

The above anecdote used the combination pattern, but you can write it in the scene or slice-of-life form.

7. Medical Anecdote You'll find anecdotes with a medical background frequently, but *Medical Economics* buys only those written by people in the medical profession, since the magazine goes to doctors and physicians. This one utilized the scene pattern.

Situation

I hospitalized a middle-aged man with a severe urinary infection. Despite massive doses of antibiotics, he hung onto life by a thread for 12 hours.

Complication

Three days after the crisis had passed I told him: "You've been very ill. In fact, it was only your strong constitution that pulled you through."

Outcome

He looked up wanly and said, "Just remember that when you make out your bill, Doc!"—JOHN NORTON, M.D.

This medical anecdote appeared in *Parish Family Digest.*§

Situation

While working as an operating room technician at the Medical Center for Federal Prisoners at Springfield, Missouri, I assisted the head nurse with an inventory of surgical equipment.

Complication

The nurse was counting instruments and with a perplexed look on her face exclaimed: "There is one syringe plunger missing."

Outcome

The surgery suite rebounded with laughter from those present when I replied, "That's the drawback working in a place like this. Once in a while you run across a crook."—WILLIAM JOE DAVIS

While *People on Parade* publishes all types of anecdote this one has a medical background.

Situation

The dentist and the psychiatrist, old friends, saw one another at a cocktail party.

§Copyright © 1980 by Our Sunday Visitor. Reprinted by permission.

Complication

"I don't know how you do it, Tom," said the dentist. "Hearing everyone's problems, frustrations and anxieties day in and day out. How can you stay so calm all the time?"

Outcome

"So, who listens?" replied the psychiatrist.—BILL HEMINGWAY

8. Business Anecdote *Reader's Digest* wants anecdotes similar to the following one for "All in a Day's Work."‖

Situation

On my first day selling Fuller brushes, I was warmly welcomed by the second housewife I called on.

Complication

It turned out that she, too, was a dealer. We had a nice chat, and by the time I was ready to leave,

Outcome

I had bought $7.50 worth of Tupperware from her, and she had bought $1.50 worth of Fuller products from me.—ELAINE B. WALLS

Under the title of "Bright Side of the Road," *Discovery* publishes amusing travel incidents that increase the fun of motoring.¶

Situation

We had stopped to eat an an expressway restaurant just off Exit 16, and we all agreed that the food was really bad.

Complication

The restaurant juke box was playing a Bobby Vinton song which included the lyrics ". . . Where did I go wrong?"

Outcome

"At Exit 16," came the voice of another unhappy customer.—BILL SIMS

"Small Talk" from *Small World* wants original anecdotes involving the owners of Volkswagens. This example follows the combination pattern.°

Situation

Joan Watkins of La Jolla, California, and her husband, in their open VW convertible, stopped at a red light.

Complication

Just opposite them was another VW convertible, top up, with a driver frantically waving. "As soon as the light changed, we pulled alongside. 'How do you get the top down?' he asked my husband. 'Just undo the latches under the sun visors,' he replied."

Outcome

'I know about the latches,' the man replied, 'but where's the button you push?' "

9. Other Markets *Expecting* buys anecdotes about happenings during pregnancy, titled "Happenings." *Roll Call* wants original, unpublished and congressionally oriented anecdotes. "Most material," the editor states, "is staff-originated or from regular contributors familiar with Congress and political topics of the day."

Gambling Times, as its title indicates, buys gambling anecdotes.

While the anecdote market remains fairly stable, you must stay alert for new publishers and old markets no longer buying. Never try to tailor a general anecdote to a specialty magazine. It will read exactly that way.

When your material fails to emerge as an anecdote, you may discover that you have a mini-article.

9

Mini-Articles

Within the last ten years, the mini-article, varying in length from 400 to 800 words, has become very popular because of the high cost of printing. Several short articles can give the reader wider coverage than one long one.

While the basic pattern will vary slightly for each type of mini-article, you can easily learn the organization. When you find an idea, simply classify it as to type of article and follow its pattern. Keep in mind that the shorter the article the more organization it requires. Some actually read as a skeleton of a longer article, so learn to limit your subject for successful selling.

These short articles also require good balance. To achieve this balance, determine the total length of your article and then apportion it to the hook, capsule sentence, development, and conclusion. Let's begin with one of the most popular and easiest features to write, the informative article.

INFORMATIVE ARTICLE

The informative article relies strongly on accurate research, around which you organize the contents. Always include a bibliography with your article to show the source of your information, whether primary or secondary. Let's study the basic mini-article for both the adult and juvenile market with a special example.

1. **Adult Article** The adult article usually opens with a hook that grabs the attention of the reader. It may vary from one sentence to a very short paragraph and should give a brief preview of the article.

Some very short articles depend on the title as a hook or else combine it with the capsule sentence. This article from *People on Parade* opens with a short hook which reinforces the title: "Drivers: Stop Helping Car Thieves."

> Careless parking habits contribute to theft of a car every 33 seconds, according to a study recently released by the Automotive Parts & Accessories Association.

As soon as you hook the reader, tell in one compact sentence what will appear in the mini-article. The capsule sentence makes a statement general enough to cover all the material in the development but specific enough to show how the writer personally reacts to the subject. Let's continue with the example.

> The APAA makes these pointers for foiling car thieves:

The development forms the body of the mini-article and comprises three fourths of the wordage. Take the capsule sentence and break it into specific statements and place them on file cards. By shuffling the cards around, you can arrange the statements in the best order—logically, geographically, dramatically, chronologically. Choose the best arrangement for your material. This development starts with leaving the car and moves on to parking it.

> Lock car doors. The APAA says four out of five cars stolen were left unlocked, and 20 percent had the key in the ignition.
> Close windows tightly to prevent a thief from reaching a lock button with a wire.
> When parking, turn wheels sharply to the right or left, making the car harder to tow.
> Try to park in well-lighted areas. . . .
> Never keep the car running while leaving the car briefly. . . .
> When parking in an attended lot, take the key ring and take the other keys with you.
> Don't keep the vehicle registration or other personal records in the car.
> Don't hide an extra key under the hood. Thieves know all the hiding places.

Many of the articles do not approach the subject as tersely as this one but will use a sentence or two of explanation, narration, or description (for a travel piece) after each statement. *Do* arrange the information so that you compress the facts to the bare essentials.

You may summarize the conclusion in a short sentence or paragraph. If you use a hook, make it and the conclusion about equal in length. With some types of information you will gives sources for more research on the subject or completely omit the conclusion. This article uses a conclusion.

> The APAA also notes that more than two-thirds of auto thefts occur at night—half occur in residential areas, so lock your car even at home.

See how easily you can write an informative mini-article.

2. Juvenile Article In the juvenile article you will simplify the information even more than for the adult one. The juvenile article frequently uses a longer and more personal hook to catch the shifting interest of the child, as in this example from *Discovery*.

> One cold autumn night I was taking out the trash. There was no moon and my eyes wandered to where the path faded into darkness, to the deep, somber shadow of the woods behind the barn. All of a sudden I froze. A huge white shadow floated silently by, not four feet away, then melted into the blackness. My muscles tensed. I strained my ears for a sound, but heard nothing. After a few moments I walked to the incinerator, dumped in the trash, and lit it. On the way back to the house I heard a high-pitched, blood-curdling shriek behind me. I shuddered in spite of myself. It was not a ghost I had met up with. The cry was that of a barn owl on its nightly prowl.

This hook runs fairly long in this article entitled "Owls," but it certainly catches the reader's interest.

The capsule sentence states:

> Owls are among the most mysterious and intriguing of birds.

115

The development for the juvenile article has fewer basic statements but contains more explanation under each. I have listed only the basic statements and one short but complete section.

> Sluggish and sleepy by day, at night the owl becomes intensely alert and watchful. . . .
> Besides being able to fly silently like a ghost, the owl can make any number of strange unearthly noises: hollow whoo-oos, wailing hoots, mournful whistles, barks, mews, snores, and clicking and snapping of the bill.
> As soon as the sun begins to rise, the owl heads for a nearby stand of pines or another secluded spot and settles himself to rest. . . .

The conclusion quickly sums up the article.

> If you hear an owl nearby, but can't locate him, hide yourself and try calling him. An owl's voice is quite easily imitated, and you may lure him quite close—maybe too close for comfort.

The article includes sketches of four different types of owls.

3. Markets Subjects for adult articles include buying habits, credit, medical advice, energy, education, tax breaks, travel, investment— any topic which touches everyday living. The juvenile magazines discuss birds, animals, pets, plants, stars, planets—subjects that more or less correlate with those taught in school.

The women's magazines *McCall's* and *Good Housekeeping* offer the largest market. In "Right Now" *McCall's* publishes a large group of mini-articles each month. In the past they have dealt with such subjects as jobs for women, laws protecting pregnant women, teen-age mumps, saccharin, nursing homes, joint custody, tips for ordering by mail, school testing, tax breaks, suntans, smoking risks— you name it. In some issues mini-articles all center on a certain theme, such as employment for women.

"The Better Way" in *Good Housekeeping* uses the same type of article and periodically develops entire sections around a central theme. Subjects discussed in the past include danger signals for debt, warts, college scholarships, tips on buying electronic games, tips on buying toys, types of insurance, types of investments, buying a fire extinguisher, mail services—the list never ends.

A number of women's magazines print back-of-the-book articles not listed in the contents. The no-listing policy results from regional advertising. Certain companies want to reach the consumers in specific geographical areas. So various magazines have certain sections where the content differs with the area. If you live in the western United States, you may get different advertising and short features than those who live in another area. These mini-articles cover travel, books for children, and other informative subjects.

The men's magazines also buy short, informative features. *Sports Afield* in "Almanac" publishes mini-articles dealing with the outdoors. "In My Experience," *American Rifleman*, wants 200 to 500 words on guns and related subjects. The national weeklies also offer a good market for short, informative pieces.

All juvenile magazines take these factual articles. The magazines published by religious presses offer markets for both adult and juvenile articles. Knowledge of your subject, first-hand or acquired through research, rates tops with any editor. Some of the same markets that publish the informative piece also buy the how-to-do-it feature.

HOW-TO-DO-IT ARTICLE

In recent years this need has greatly expanded for both the juvenile and the adult markets. The how-to-do-it article differs from the informative feature in that it involves the reader in the action of a craft and stresses the *how* of the task. This mini-article follows the basic pattern: problem hook, capsule sentence, material, directions, and conclusion. The long pattern uses all steps. Most markets, however, buy all patterns, so your material will determine the best one.

1. **Long Pattern** The long form of the article starts with the problem, as does this one on Christmas ornaments from *The Mother Earth News*.

Problem Hook

How would you like to decorate your Yuletide tree with lovely homemade ornaments this year?

Capsule Sentence

There's nothing to it. . . .

Material

just gather the family together, get some yarn and sticks (anything from pieces of dowel to small twigs will do), and make a party out of the project.

Directions

Cross two of your sticks (cut to whatever length you want), and wire or tie them together as shown in Fig. 1. Then hold the struts between your thumb and forefinger and—leaving a loose end three inches long—wrap three to four turns of yarn around the cross's intersection. Knot off these "anchor" strands and start to weave the yarn onto the frame . . . making a hook around each stick as you go (Fig. 3).

When your decoration is as large as you want it to be, tie a knot . . . to the last wrapped strand.

You can vary the designs of your ornaments in several ways . . .

If you'd like a little "sparkle" in your holiday, why not paint designs on the finished ornaments. . . .

Conclusion

You'll find that making your own Christmas tree decorations is downright habit-forming. Who knows, after you wrap up a few of these yarn ornaments you might want to string some popcorn or cranberries, and have a completely home-decorated tree that'll bring the "good old days" right into your living room!—ALICE ROCHELLE FULLER

This pattern usually has some sketches or pictures that give further directions to the reader.

The men's article will combine the hook and the capsule sentence and interweave the material into the action for a shorter version of the long pattern. The juvenile piece makes the instructions very simple.

2. Short Pattern In the short form the title may serve as the hook and the capsule sentence, so that the article begins by listing the material. "How to Make a Candle Flashlight," from *Living for Self-Sufficiency* in "Notebook," *Applewood Journal,* illustrates this pattern.

Material

For this you need an old can, about one-pound size or bigger, with the top and bottom removed.

Directions

Then cut a cross with a sharp knife in the middle side, and push your candle up through the center of the cross until the wick lies almost exactly in center of the can. Make two small holes in top and fit a wire handle. . . .

Conclusion

It gives something like a lantern beam, and only the strongest of winds out-of-doors will ever blow it out. One of them can save you a lot of flashlight batteries when you go out to put the hens to bed.

The pattern appears frequently in the men's outdoor magazines or juvenile market because of the brevity.

3. Step-by-Step Pattern By using sketches or pictures, you eliminate words. To make the text easy for the reader to follow, you place each step in a separate paragraph, as in "Cluster Curls" from *Doll World Omnibook.*°

Hook and Capsule Sentence

Cluster curls are easy to make and are a nice change from the braided or straight hairdos usually seen on rag dolls.

Material

I used Dazzle yarn. This yarn is very soft and makes lovely curls.

Directions

Measure length of hair needed, and cut a piece of cardboard as

°Reprinted by permission of the House of White Birches, Inc., Seabrook, N.H.

shown. Wrap lengths of yarn around piece . . . stick down center . . . leave (ends) in loops.

Attach hairpiece to doll head down center part.

Tie at each side, to make "pony tails." . . .

Separate about 6 strands of yarn. Cut a 5″ piece of yarn and slip through loops at end of hair. Tie in a single knot.

Roll yarn over knot. . . .

Conclusion

After all curls are made, arrange and fluff for desired effect.— BARBARA ARMSTRONG

In "Crafty Critters," *Make It With Leather* actually does nothing more than write captions for the sketches.

Material Needed

Scissors, Scrap Garment Suede, Awl, Craftool Segma Snap Setter, 1 Glove Snap, No. 2 and 4 Round Drive Punch, Acrylic Dye or Fabric Pens, Needle and Waxed Thread.

The writer, Carl Fultz, lists these directions for the coin-purse pattern.

Directions

Trace pattern onto leather. . . .

Fold the leather into the coin-purse shape and make certain your stitching holes match. . . .

Practice setting snaps on scrap before attempting it on your project.

Stitch up both sides of the purse using needle and waxed thread. Begin at bottom and work to the top. . . .

This magazine also buys short how-to-do-it articles under the title of "Scrap Bin Projects." While this one follows the step-by-step pattern, it uses only one illustration.

4. Narrative Pattern This pattern appears more often in the men's magazines. Narration reduces the number of words and gives a chattiness to the presentation.

"Painless Hook Removal," from "How It's Done" in *Field and Stream* provides a good example of this technique.

Hook

Sooner or later nearly every fisherman becomes the victim of his own hook . . . he has had the painful responsibility of removing one from a buddy, his child, or even his dog. . . .

Material and Capsule Sentence

There is a painless technique of hook removal. . . . The only tool required is a 2-foot piece of strong (15-pound or more) monofilament line.

Directions

The line is doubled, then looped around the imbedded hook. The eye of the hook is pressed firmly down on the flesh of the victim so that the hook stands arched upward. Then the doubled monofilament is gripped firmly and given a good hard yank. The hook flies painlessly out. . . .

Conclusion

When the eye of the hook is held down, the yank on the line rolls the barb right out under the flesh . . . painlessly.—s. m. RUMMEL

Hunting Dog Magazine has a section, called "Pro's Tip," similar to the one in *Field and Stream*. It uses the same narrative style of presentation.

SELF-HELP ARTICLE

The mini-self-help article may develop in several ways: a solution to a common problem in daily living, a step-by-step approach to self-improvement, or a spiritual uplift to chase "the blues." All of these follow the pattern of hook, capsule sentence, development, and conclusion.

1. **Problem-Solution** In this approach to self-help you choose a problem shared by many, such as moving to a new town, taking

care of elderly parents, getting acquainted in a new city, and so on. In *Good News* each issue deals with how to have family devotions, as in "Here a Little . . . There a Little," by Paul and Ann Morell.

Problem Hook

Traditional family devotions haven't worked well for our family! If you think that means we have quit trying, you are wrong! . . .

Capsule Sentence

"Here a little, there a little" describes better what has taken place at our house through the years.

Development

Sometimes it would include the whole family—other times only mom and children. . . . Often I share a Scripture that has been meaningful to me during my quiet time. Some days we read the Upper Room or Daily Blessing.

Now when older children return home, or when there are guests in the home, often we have Bible reading and prayer just before bedtime.

Conclusion

Nahum 2:1 reminds us that "The shatterer has come up against you. Man the ramparts; watch the road; gird your loins; collect all your strength." Shatterers will always attempt to halt family devotions. We must daily gird up our loins, collect our strength, and proceed with love and determination for the spiritual nurture of our families.

2. Self-Improvement For this type of self-help article, the national weeklies, such as *National Enquirer* and *The Star*, offer the best market. "How to Face and Deal with Rejection" appeared in *The Star*.

Problem Hook

Rejections in work, social and even love situations can often be overcome and turned into acceptance, says a leading psychotherapist.

But sometimes the best thing we can do is try to understand the reason . . . to live with it, said Thomas Ruggiero. . . .

Capsule Sentence

Ruggiero has these suggestions for dealing with rejection:

Development

Rejection at Work

Talk with other person. . . .

Seek a third person's help. If you feel the rejection is interfering with your effectiveness—whether at work or in a social group or club—you may have to call on someone else for help.

Don't let the situation get out of hand. . . .

Rejection by a Superior

Avoid seeking total approval. . . .

Don't pursue the wrong people. . . .

Conclusion

Avoid being a "love addict." Some people want the whole world to accept them . . . When it doesn't, they continually feel rejected and dejected. Expecting total acceptance from the world is not realistic.

Each of the points in the development has one or two sentences of expansion. Keep paragraphs in such articles very short and to the point, for these pieces have no excess words.

3. Spiritual Uplift This type of article will run either very short or else up to 800 words. The narrative style has a talking-to-the-reader effect. This example from *Christian Adventurer,* "My Day Is Today," shows how to create the spiritual uplift.

Problem Hook and Capsule Sentence

There are two days in the week upon which and about which I never worry: two carefree days, kept sacredly free from fear and apprehension.

Development

One of these days is Yesterday. Yesterday . . . has passed forever beyond the reach of my recall. . . .

Save for the beautiful memories, sweet and tender, that linger like the perfume of roses in the heart of the day that is gone, I have nothing to do with Yesterday. It was mine; it is God's.

The other day I do not worry about is Tomorrow. . . . Tomorrow—
it is God's day.

There is left for myself, then, but one day of the week—Today. . . .
It is not the experience of Today that drives men mad, it is the re-
morse for something that happened Yesterday, the dread of what Tomorrow may disclose.

Conclusion

These are God's days. Leave them with Him. Therefore I think,
and I do, and I journey, but one day at a time; that is the easy way.
That day is man's day. Nay, rather that is our day, God's and mine.
While faithfully and dutifully we run our course, and work our appointed task on that day of ours, God, the Almighty and the all-
loving, takes care of Yesterday and Tomorrow.

The sentences omitted under each of the development statements
merely enlarge on the thoughts already expressed. While this one
has a religious overtone, the mini-self-help article need not. But it
must chase "the blues" away.

You will find another kind of inspirational message in short devo-
tional articles like the ones *Parish Family Digest* publishes. The
opening paragraph shows a problem situation, the second makes an
application to life and religion, and the last provides a message for
living. A number of religious publications use these.

PROFILE

The profile filler stresses the individual and what he thinks, says, or
does. The facet of the personality you emphasize depends on the
religious or secular market. Specialty magazines want profiles of
people in their fields of endeavor—for instance, a leather worker for
a magazine on leather crafts.

The profile may show a little-known person who helps others, a
writer who protests, or an artist who works with the disabled.

1. **Worthy Person** *Guideposts* wants a one-page filler for "The
Quiet People." The featured person must help others but go about it
quietly and with good results. By all means, get the consent of the

person before you submit the profile and send along a copy of this permission and a picture to the editor. Louise Burgess wrote this one on Glenn Weinschenk for *Guideposts.*†

Contribution

The elderly lady had just settled into the front seat of the bus parked outside the Wesley Palms Retirement Home in San Diego, California, when she jumped up and exclaimed in dismay, "I can't go! I forgot my purse!"

"Do you need some money?" asked the driver.

"Well, I've got a little shopping to do. . . ."

"What do you need—five, ten dollars?"

The woman, a newcomer to the Home, and literally a stranger, gratefully accepted the loan of five dollars for her shopping needs.

The driver's name is Glenn Weinschenk,

Proof

and for five years this scene and others similar to it have occurred on his bus. . . . Glenn's bus serves the needs of the elderly folk who may wish to travel into town to shop or attend Sunday services or weekly activities of their church. . . .

It's not an infrequent occurrence for Glenn to drive several blocks out of his way. . . .

The quiet, kindly man has learned to understand the needs and eccentricities of his elderly riders. . . .

Glenn's patience never seems to give out.

Before coming to Wesley Palms, Glenn drove a city bus in Flint, Michigan. By popular vote . . . he was voted best driver for two successive three-month periods.

Dominant Trait

Glenn Weinschenk brings to his daily job an extra ingredient over and above efficient work; he brings loving concern for those he serves.

You need not show the contribution in action, but you may summarize it. Then you prove your statement by giving specific incidents. At the end you focus on the dominant trait.

2. Protest While a number of magazines want protest features, you must keep them short. In the protest the writer opens with a situation many people suffer through and do nothing about. The writer, in first-person viewpoint, summarizes the situation, gives the arguments for his or her position, and ends with the message of the protest. *Lady's Circle* bought this one.

Protest

I'm sounding off about one of the ways TV is misused in American homes today. There is nothing I dislike more than being invited to a friend's home only to find that I am expected to watch TV, with conversation occurring only during commercials.

Argument

First of all, this is a breach of good manners. . . .

I feel that what little time we have for our friends should be spent in enjoying good old-fashioned *talk*.

Since children quickly adopt the habits of adults, we should provide a good example in how we treat our invited guests. . . . We simply do not allow the TV to intrude.

Message

We cherish our friends too much to have an evening dominated by a picture tube.—MRS. D. M. YOUNG

3. Profile by Quotation What a person says projects his character and can often reveal a timeless philosophy of life. The following quotation comes from Richard Rodgers in "Points to Ponder" in *Reader's Digest.*‡

I am in favor of the love song. I do not think the honorable profession of song writing can flourish without it, and I have strong doubts that love can flourish without it either.

The songwriter can create the appropriate mood, bring back memories, ease a pain (or prolong one). He can supply words for the tongue-tied and lift the hearts of the lonely. Nearly every day I receive at least one letter from someone telling me how much a song of mine meant to him.

And I would like to think that love songs—of all themes and tempos—do something to dispel the conflicts and tensions that are so much a part of our daily lives, and help create bonds of sympathy. After all, as someone said, nobody has yet written a hit song about hate.—*The Saturday Evening Post*

Most markets require a published source, such as a book or magazine.

The *American Dane* magazine needs similar quotations, but about people with a Danish background. The magazine attributes this quotation to the Danish-American industrialist, William S. Knudsen.

> An assistant rushed into Mr. Knudsen's office one day very upset because a certain report was missing.
> "There are two kinds of reports," Knudsen said calmly. "One says you can't do it. The other says it has been done. The first one is no good. The second kind you don't need."—WAYNE A. SYMONDS

"Personal Glimpses" in *Reader's Digest* needs quotations that show an unknown facet of a person's character. *Book Digest* invites readers to submit excerpts of 150 words or less of either wit or wisdom taken from any book except anthologies. *Decision* also uses this type of filler, grouping several quotations together. *Do* include with any excerpt the source, author, title, publisher (hardcover or paperback), and page number(s).

HUMOR ARTICLE

The humor article may focus on the actions of a single individual or compile a list of humorous incidents.

1. Party of One When you focus on the actions of a single person, you may follow the informative, how-to-do-it, self-help, or profile pattern. This example, "Wit Stop" in *People on Parade*, reverses the pattern of the self-help article.

Problem

> It all started with women's suffrage in 1921. After winning the right to vote, women continued to fight for other equalities. But even

as they expand their horizons into fields long dominated by men, most women have not yet indicated a desire to abandon motherhood. And with new opportunities added to old responsibilities, their lives have become complex.

Capsule Sentence

Doing all they seek to do requires a kind of supermother.

Development

Football is suited more to men's physical attributes, but Dad's playing golf and the two boys need a tight end. . . .

Little Bradley loves snakes, lizards, frogs, and spiders. Try to overcome your fears. . . .

This was the day you desperately needed a rest for that splitting headache. But little Angela comes in, crushed that her friends have found someone new to play with. . . .

You are the only family on the block with a swimming pool. . . .

—DICK HARRIS

A cartoon illustrates each of these situations. Note that you stop with the reader wanting more of the humor. Let your readers collaborate with you and write in their own incidents—they probably can. Good humor must know when to stop.

2. Collective When you bind together a collection of related incidents from several sources, you should put a binder sentence at the beginning to show the relationship. In "When I die . . ." from *People on Parade*, Edward R. Walsh collects the dying words of a number of people.

Binder

One might expect that life's last lines would be serious and somber. Well, it's not necessarily so. Many a soul spirited into the Great Beyond had muttered words more laughable than laudable, more puckish than practical.

Incidents

When English humorist Sydney Smith was told he had just drunk a dose of ink by mistake, he retorted: "Then bring me all the blotting paper there is in the house."

The article continues to quote the last comments of people from all walks of life.

Writing these mini-articles gives you practice for the longer ones. While these articles stick to the facts, the personal-experience variety adds drama.

*10
Mini-Personal
Experience

The mini-personal experience has grown in popularity because it reflects interesting emotional facts about human nature and provides good reader identification. Truth always proves more fascinating than fiction. Keep the time span of the experience very short or vague and emphasize characterization and action in first-person viewpoint.

PATTERN

The mini-experience opens with a *problem* that shows the writer in a negative light. In the effort to solve the problem the person makes a positive change and states a *message*—a universal truth—that may help the reader.

1. **Problem** In addition to showing a negative image of the person, the statement of the problem usually relates why it developed. Hold this to one sentence but give enough information for the reader to understand and care about the solution to the problem. The setting may or may not affect the problem. The setting in this experience from "Turning Point," *Grit*, actually causes the problem.

Problem

I was furious as I viewed the beer cans, paper cups and plates, and other litter on the ground around the picnic tables where I sat. . . .

I had stopped at the lake-side picnic area for a few moments of prayer and meditation.

2. Solution As the writer works through to a solution and to taking specific action, the person slowly changes—the image becomes positive.

Solution

I opened my pocket edition of the New Testament and began to read. But my eyes kept wandering to the trash-covered grass. And my prayerful mood began to change to anger.

Then a voice seemed to say to me, "If this litter disturbs you so much, why don't you do something about it?" . . .

Moments later I had begun . . . my most unusual worship period. As I picked up trash, I realized my bitterness was lessening.

. . . as I worked . . . I was talking to God.

3. Change and Message The action you take brings about your change of character and offers the opportunity for you to summarize what you have learned—the message.

Change and Message

As I dropped the last can into a trash container I gazed across the lake. . . . So beautiful was the sight that I began to hum, then broke into a song of praise. . . . I could not help thanking God for the beauty He has made for us.

That experience taught me that when I encounter things in this world that are ugly—such as hate, greed, and selfishness—maybe I can do something about them, even in my own small way, and make my corner of the world a little better.

In writing the mini-experience use all the techniques for developing character and action given previously. When the editor limits you to under three hundred words, narrate the action. If you can write five hundred words, depict the action in short scenes, incidents, and dialogue for more dramatics.

Expect two difficulties in writing this type of experience: you start writing before you know the message, and you fail to eliminate facts that have little or no relation to the message. Learn to write the message first and select the facts to support it.

TYPES OF MINI-EXPERIENCES

Markets such as national weeklies, confession magazines and religious publications select a title and request that you write about it. From time to time the editors will change the title when they fail to get continuing submittals. You must keep up with the changing titles and must fit your experience to them.

1. **Religious Experience** A number of markets want religion to play a dominant role in the solution of the problem, as it did in the opening example. The writer may pray for himself or herself, or for someone else.

Guideposts wants a mini-experience where prayer points the way to the solution—when God speaks in a whisper—for "Fragile Moments." °

Problem

I was engaged to be married, yet my mother was a chronic invalid and because I was the only unmarried daughter, our family felt it was my responsibility to stay and care for her. My fiancé was impatient and I was confused.

Solution

One evening I went into my church to pray about this problem. While in meditation, my eyes lifted to our beautiful stained glass windows. But the church was only dimly lit: . . . The windows were but a jumble of varicolored glass—formless, meaningless, chaotic.
. . . But the glimmer of a thought broke through.

The next morning I hurried back to the church. What a transformation the sunlight made on the stained glass windows! The light shone through each fragment of color, . . . changing the formless shapes of the night before into a radiant pattern . . .

Change and Message

and in the same moment, a light broke into my confused mind. I was in a state of mental darkness because I was relying solely on my own powers. It is God who supplied the light for our lives. He can take out

°Copyright © 1967 by Guideposts Associates, Inc., Carmel, N.Y. Reprinted by permission.

shapeless designs and ambitions, and through us give them direction and purpose. But first we must give Him ourselves.

For several years, I cared for my mother until she passed away. My fiancé wouldn't wait. God knew best, though, because He eventually led me to a man who has been a truly wonderful husband.
—WILMA MARTINSON

In this example the writer used major-character viewpoint. In "The Open Door" from *Catholic Digest*, the viewpoint may vary between the major or minor character. All of the experiences under this heading relate how the writer became a Catholic.

Problem

My newly found friend from out of town needed a guide to show her the way to the cathedral here in Columbus, Ohio. I took her. She was a convert, and wished to review her instructions with a priest.

Solution

. . . I found myself accompanying her . . . twice a week indefinitely.

. . . I had become too interested to end the visits. I began instructions on my own. . . .

Meanwhile I met a Catholic man who eventually became my husband. I finished my instructions, and was baptized.

Change and Message

Of course when I was married, my matron of honor could be none other than the girl who had shown me the way, via the cathedral, to a new life in the church.—BETTY GEBHARDT

Gospel Carrier wants the experience to have a clear Christian message.

Problem

Dr. Malan of Geneva, on a trip to Paris, fell into conversation with a chap who began to reason with him about Christianity. The Doctor answered every argument with a quotation from the Scriptures. . . .

At last he [his companion] turned away. "Don't you see. I don't believe your Bible! What's the use of quoting it to me?" he screamed.

But the only reply was another thrust, "If ye believe not that I am He, ye shall die in your sins."

Solution

Years afterward, Dr. Malan one day tore open a letter. . . . "You took the Sword of the Spirit and stabbed me through and through," it read.

Change and Message

"And every time I tried to parry the blade . . . you simply gave me another stab. You made me feel I was not fighting you, but God."

At the close Dr. Malan recognized the name of his Paris-bound companion of years before.

The editor of *Gospel Carrier* urges that you read several issues before you submit.

2. Thematic Experience *Catholic Digest* buys three different thematic experiences in which the title carries the message. "The Perfect Assist" experience tells about help from a friend or a stranger. This example illustrates this theme.

Problem

We had stopped at a lovely family restaurant for dinner. . . . Right in the middle of the delightful meal, my husband looked suddenly stricken, and he asked softly, "Do you have any money? My wallet is on the dresser at home. . . ." I had only 37¢!

Solution

After a hushed, frantic discussion my husband left the table to find the manager. . . . We were a good 50 miles from home with food before us and no possible way of paying for it.

Change

My husband returned to the table. "It's perfectly OK," he sighed with relief. "I'll send him a check in the morning." . . . as we were getting ready to leave, my husband reached into his pocket and came out with a handful of change. "I thought you didn't have any money," I whispered. "I didn't," he grinned as he slipped $1 in change under the edge of his plate. "The manager gave it to me—for the tip!"—ANN QUINLAN

Do you recall the time a stranger or a friend gave you "The Perfect Assist?"

"People Are Like That" recounts a true event that illustrates the instinctive goodness of human nature.

Problem

During the Depression, when my sister was diagnosed as a diabetic, father was working eight to ten days a month at most. Faced with the dilemma of no money and the need for a regular supply of insulin, mother swallowed her stiff German pride and approached the manager of our only drugstore.

Solution

The store belonged to a chain which had a rigid policy of no charge accounts. Mother explained her need, promised to charge nothing but insulin, and honestly admitted that some months their return would amount to no more than a dollar or two.

In a crisp, businesslike way the manager assured her that her credit was perfectly acceptable and

Change

for years we carried the charge account. Sometimes it was difficult— the clerks keep repeating the no-charge-account policy—but the manager always intervened.

It was many years before we realized that the no credit rule was still in effect; the charge account was with the manager, not the store.—ANN WINGER

Notice the long time lapse before the writer and the family learned the truth. This time lapse establishes the instinctive goodness of the manager and shows the action as more than a quick good turn.

In "Hearts Are Trumps," we see how unseeking kindness earned a reward, or bread cast upon the water comes back.

Problem

A few years ago, when San Diego factories suddenly decreased production, thousands of people were left unemployed. For men past 60, like my husband, there were almost no jobs available. Fortunately, my husband found work in an all-night filling station. It was a risky job. Night holdups were becoming frequent, and he was constantly afraid of being attacked.

Solution

Experienced with the hardships of unemployment, my husband found it difficult to refuse customers who were out of work the gas they needed. One night he loaned a quarter from his own pocket to a stranger who was hurrying to see his ailing father.

Change

Then one dark night. . . . A bandit slugged him on the head, fracturing his skull. He might have been left lying for hours on the cold concrete floor—but for a grateful stranger. When he regained consciousness in the hospital, my husband learned that he owed his life to a man who had stopped at the station to pay him back his quarter.— ADA BREISE CROMER

3. Humorous Experience Several markets want the humorous experience typical of "My Funniest Moment" from *Grit*. These stress only the laughter and omit a character change and message.

Problem

I taught English in a small county school and was given extra duty of putting on plays. We had a shoestring budget. . . . We had to depend on imagination and ingenuity instead of money.

Solution

I was extremely proud of one play. It was about olden days and attics were combed for clothing and furniture until the stage was really effective.

A snow scene was one of the most important ones in the play, and we found perfect snow—soap flakes. . . .

A student hidden from sight sat on a rafter, sifting the flakes downward.

Outcome

Busy backstage, I suddenly heard a roar of laughter from the audience even though it was a serious moment in the play. . . . The student had dropped the soap box.—PHYLLIS JORDAN

For *Grit* "each humorous story must be true, from your own experience, and not published previously." The editor allows you 300 words.

Midnight/Globe in "Dear Suzie" used this humorous experience.

Problem

I am retired, but I do odd carpenter jobs. . . .

One day I was asked to fix a fruit and vegetable stand.

I was squatting down below the stand that held some honey dew melons at the time when an elderly woman with poor eye sight approached.

The next thing I knew she was stroking my head and squeezing it a little, while telling the clerk that she wanted "That melon" because it had a nice shape and was very firm.

Solution

The clerk looked and started laughing, while telling the customer it was my head. You see, I'm completely bald.

Outcome

The clerk . . . never fails to greet me with, "How do you do, Honey Dew?"—FRED MILLHAM

4. Everyday Living Experience The national weeklies, confession magazines, and religious publications want experiences that might happen to anyone. The confession and religious markets stress the stronger character-change and message. *Capper's Weekly* buys "angel" stories for "In the Heart of the Home." Most people will find an angel around to give help in time of need.

Problem

They say everyone has an unseen guardian angel who sort of helps keep us from injury, but I met an angel once who was quite visible.

I had left my car on a small Minnesota farm and rode with my son to visit a relative in a Minneapolis hospital. The next night I returned by bus, picked up my car and proceeded homeward.

It had begun to snow. . . . As I got beyond the city limits, I found visibility almost nonexistent.

Solution

On I drove at a snail's pace, seeing many cars on the roadside or in the ditch. . . .

A truck followed me for a mile or two. . . . blinking his headlights. He passed and pulled to the side of the road, stopped and waved me down.

Naturally I feared violence. He showed me a card . . . to assure me he meant no harm.

Change and Message

"Lady," he said, "you will not make it to your destination. If you will let me drive your car, my partner will pilot us with the truck."

Needless to say I accepted his kind offer. . . . He refused any pay, but after my letter to his company telling of his courtesy, he received commendation.

So if I never meet another angel, I certainly met one that cold December night.

An experience can bring a sob to your throat. The editor of *Guideposts* states that he wants "good shorts of two or three paragraphs. Short back-cover features sometimes have a seasonal flavor. These are filler-length, usually." "The Priceless Reward" comes from this market.[†]

Problem

Growing up the youngest of five children, I was never asked to wear hand-me-downs or second-hand clothes, for in our home we felt fortunate to have anything to wear at all. My mother, who had been widowed during the Depression of the early twenties and was our sole provider, would take the clothes that we were given, mend them, restyle and starch them until they were beautiful.

One day my oldest brother brought home a suitcase that somebody had left on the sidewalk near the bus station in town. Inside were a lot of what Mama described as "fine clothes" and I was thrilled to discover that the dresses would fit me. But my mother said, "No, they belong to another little girl and we must give them back."

Solution

The next morning she sent my brother on a five-mile walk to the bus station where he found that the loss had been reported. About two weeks later, we received a letter from the owners of the suitcase. "Didn't they send a reward?" I asked.

Change and Message

And my mother said, quite simply, "Yes, baby, they did. They said 'thank you.'"—ELIZABETH LASHLEY

From a sad experience may come the inspiration to face your own problem. This experience appeared in *Parish Family Digest*.‡

Problem

We own a nursing home. . . . Because we live on the grounds my children become "grandkids" to the patients. . . . "Foxy" Roxy, my seven-year-old daughter, was a special favorite.

When she developed cancer, it was devastating to all of us. . . .

Solution

I had to be away from the nursing home to care for her for the last two weeks before her death.

I went back to the home with new impressions of what it is like to be terminally ill. . . . in every patient's room the story had been the same. "Why couldn't I have died in her place. . . ."

Change and Message

My answer, when I could speak through my grateful tears was, "Who knows what God had in mind for her in Heaven, and who knows what He has in mind for us, here. There must be something more He wants us to do, or He wants to give us before He takes us."

. . . Roxy's death had made such a difference in the home, drawing people together in friendship, making everyone more tolerant of foibles. Indeed Roxy's death preached a poignant sermon.—MARTHA J. BECKMAN

Sometimes an experience can expose the foibles of the writer as he takes a long look at himself. "A New View of Housecleaning" by Elaine Minton comes from *Home Life*.

Problem

"Cleanliness is next to godliness" should have been carved in wood and hung over the front door of our home. . . . Mother worked from early in the morning until late at night to keep us and our house clean. . . .

Even though as a child, I complained, I adopted my mother's standards when I became a homemaker. . . . But, with the births of our two boys, the housework increased, the time to do it decreased, and I became frustrated.

‡ Copyright © 1979 by Our Sunday Visitor. Reprinted by permission.

Solution

. . . I realized that the responsibility I felt to keep the house clean was interfering with my family's enjoyment. . . . Do you know that "Cleanliness is next to godliness" is not in the Bible?

Change and Theme

But this verse is: "An empty stable stays clean—but there is no income from an empty stable." (Prov. 14:4 TLB)

This verse helped me rethink my cleaning standards. I still keep my house orderly. . . . Perhaps when my children are older, my house will be cleaner . . . I'm having too much fun with my family.

My mother recently reaffirmed my new priorities when she told me: "If I had it to do over, I would spend more time with my children. They grow up and leave, but the housework will wait."

5. Outdoors Experience *Outdoor Life* has an adventure experience called "This Happened to Me." An illustrator puts the piece into six or seven picture frames. The adventure may deal with a wild-animal attack, such as a charge by a wild elephant or an injured buck. Sometimes the adventure tells of mountain climbing or getting trapped in rough seas while in a fishing boat. Most of the experiences involve a life-and-death crisis. When you write your experience, try to picture the action in six frames as you apply the basic pattern. Men have dominated the adventure market, but women have begun to play a larger role.

Under the general title of "Would You Believe?" *Bowhunter Magazine* publishes short personal experiences like the example below.

Problem

I'm fifteen years old and have been a bowhunter for six years. . . .

Last summer I built myself a tree stand over a well-used game trail. . . . For three Mondays in a row . . . I saw a 10-point buck which always managed to keep just out of bow range.

On my fourth hunt I had just gotten into my tree when I saw a spike buck coming down the trail. When he got within 10 yards of me I nailed him through his spine and he fell in his tracks. By this time I was so highly excited . . . I dropped the others [arrows] from my quiver and they spilled onto the ground below.

Before I had a chance to . . . retrieve my arrows, I heard . . . the big 10-pointer heading for my tree. He stopped in front of the dead spike and snorted. . . . Then he charged the deer I had just shot.

Solution

. . . even if I could have taken a second deer legally, I didn't have any arrows. . . . I let out with the loudest yell I could manage. . . . The 10-pointer bounded away!

Outcome

I climbed down and set out to find my father. . . . I wanted him to help me dress my spike buck. . . . Father was busy field-dressing the 10-pointer which I had scared away from my tree.—DAVE WORTH

Runner's World buys experiences of joggers for "Reader's Forum." "A Shoe-In," by Carol Tracy, relates a rather unusual experience.

Problem

The other evening I was grinding out my daily six miles at the local high school track. . . . Half a dozen boys were gathered in the shadows at one end of the stadium. One of them would leave the group. . . . He'd return . . . and another boy would break away and rip off a 440. I put the watch on one of them and caught him in a decent 66-flat. The others were all in the same range.

I wondered why only one boy ran at a time; . . . then it dawned on me—they had only one pair of shoes. Suddenly, I was depressed.

Solution

On balance, we runners are a pretty affluent group.

Most of us simply toss our old shoes into the trash can. Some of us give them to various charity organizations. . . .

Change and Message

I now give my old shoes to the local Boy's Club with explicit instructions that they find their way onto young running feet. . . .

Perhaps local running clubs or AAU chapters would undertake to act as distribution points; but either way, I encourage other runners to give more thought to the proper "retirement" of their old shoes. Passing my shoes on to a young runner who can't afford his or her own seems a much more personal expression of my love for a sport that has given me so much pleasure.

6. Military Experience For *Ladycom* magazine the editor states that "fillers, in most cases, should reflect experiences of the audience, i.e., military wives." "Good-bye Friend," by Judith McCowell, illustrates this type of experience.

Problem

We're leaving now. Three busy years have rushed away, and now the tour is done. I don't think I can stand to say good-bye. My friend next door is everything a friend should be. . . .

Our friendship didn't blossom overnight, . . . or arrive by magic. First, there were the casual hellos and little chats . . . I realize how lucky we have been to live so close and be so close and hardly ever get on each other's nerves. . . .

No one-way street connects my friend next door and me, for friendship flows both ways. . . .

How can I say good-bye to this good friend and drive away to start again at some new base, to feel again that lost feeling I have known so well. . . .

Here comes my friend. Lord, help me not to cry. How must she feel, the one who's left behind?

Solution

Quickly we hug, and she hands me crackers and cheese to eat in the car: somehow we say our last good-bye and drive away. . . .

We'll write often for a while and maybe even call a few times. . . .

Change and Message

But our next-door days are over, a precious time that will never return.

The friendship, though, we'll keep, a cherished part of both of us that we can take out and examine when we need to, or simply treasure deep inside us all our days, below the stream of conscious thought.

7. Strange-Phenomena Experience *Beyond Reality Magazine* purchases accounts of unexplained phenomena. Like "The Ghost in Seat DD113," they show a situation and comment on its unreality.

Situation

Seat DD113 of the Woodstock, Ill. Opera House is often occupied by more than just an occasional opera buff. This particular seat is often said to contain the spirit of a beautiful young woman who hung herself in the very belfry of the theater around the turn of the century.

Elvira, as she is known, is frequently seen in her favorite seat, DD113, by the performers, moaning and groaning her disapproval of particular rehearsals.

Comment

Spirits who have died an unhappy or violent death are known to haunt the vicinity of their demise, and Elvira, the blonde beauty, is no exception. Instead of haunting the belfry where her suicide was committed, however, she seems to be attracted to a particular seat. Perhaps the cause of her death was because of an unsuccessful love affair and seat DD113 was her lover's favorite, or maybe the seat was the choice of her rival. Whatever the cause, it doesn't seem to bother Illinois theater goers. Seat DD113 is the most popular seat in the house, says opera house director Doug Rankin. Elvira may just be waiting for either her lover or her rival to once again return, and take that destined seat.

Fate also has a strong interest in any unexplained phenomena. Many of these come from newspaper accounts. *Midnight/Globe* often publishes articles on such experiences under the title of "Your Story," but it also features other types of experiences. The experience of ESP dominates a number of these stories.

Situation

My 19-year-old son, Glenn, was admitted to Bexar County Hospital in San Antonio for acute leukemia.

About 6 P.M., the doctors told me to go home because there was nothing more I could do there.

That night, I was lying in bed and thinking about Glenn. I remembered how he would toss pebbles at my window after a date so I would unlock the door and let him in.

I finally fell asleep and then I awoke with a start—I heard the sound of pebbles against the window and Glenn say: "I'm home, Mom. Please open the door."

I ran downstairs and opened the door but no one was there.

Then I remembered that Glenn was in the hospital.

As I got back into bed, I noticed the time was 3:30 A.M.

Comment

When I went to the hospital later that day, doctors told me that Glenn had passed the crisis point at 3:30 A.M.

And when I finally saw my son, he said that he concentrated on me during the night . . . to let me know that he was going to be all right.—EMMA MEUTH

Some of the experiences under "Narrow Escape" in *Grit* also tell of strange coincidences. For example, because of a mix-up in travel reservations, a couple had to take a later ship instead of the *Andrea Doria*, which sank.

Nothing intrigues the reader more than ghost stories, unexplained quirks of fate, or strange phenomena. Take a look at your life and see if you might have such an experience to share, but make sure you tell the true story. Editors have a way of recognizing the real experience. These mini-experiences of all types have become so popular that many editors urge readers to contribute longer ones.

11*
Reader-Contribution
Features

Frequently, the editor of a magazine will place a short note at the
end of a feature and ask the reader to share opinions or experiences.
Usually, the invitation will give you the amount paid, the desired
length, and possibly the general subject. To sell the market you must
analyze the features for specific subjects, viewpoint, characterization, and style of writing. These features vary in length from 500 to
2,000 words, but always write the length the editor suggests. The
subject matter and organization will enable you to group these features into categories.

PERSONAL PROBLEM

The personal problem shares with the reader a situation that might
happen to anyone. Shy away from glamorous subjects and out-of-
this-world solutions to the problem. In short, try to work within the
realm of what could happen to any person under the circumstances.
Naturally, you will dramatize the information with short-story techniques; but don't dramatize too much or you will lose the ring of
truth.

1. Pattern The pattern will follow these divisions: problem, chronology, crisis, and conclusion. In the first two or three paragraphs,
tell the reader the problem. Usually, you must narrate this briefly
because of the word limit. You may start the problem at the onset or
at a dramatic point later on. By all means show yourself with a
negative attitude toward the situation.

Regardless of where you start with the problem, you show it

grows worse chronologically. If you start at a high point in the problem, you then go back to the beginning and show its development.

At the crisis point of the struggle, you find the positive solution. This brings about a character change from a negative to a positive attitude.

In the conclusion you talk with the reader and briefly state how your life has changed. Generally, you have solved the problem or at least recognized the best solution, and will put it into effect. Tell the reader in one sentence, a theme, what you have learned from these events. Let's apply this pattern to specific markets.

2. Markets The *Ladies' Home Journal* regularly publishes "It's Not Easy to Be A Woman Today!" Recent issues have dealt with adopting a baby, divorce, face-lifts, maturing, finding a liberated man, having a baby, going back to work, and becoming a housewife.

The editor states: "We'd like to know how you, as a woman, are facing your own life and problems. . . . Tell us how you are solving a specific situation, large or small, that represents the changing times in which women live today."

Let's briefly analyze one of the articles on a woman whose husband wanted a divorce to marry a neighbor and best friend.

Problem

My husband wanted a divorce, so I gave him one. But I felt sorry for myself. (*negative attitude*)

Chronology

I felt very lonely, so I surrounded myself with new friends who shared my problem.

To add interest to my life, I began some creative activities.

I gave more attention to my children.

Crisis

My friends introduced me to a new man.

Conclusion

I learned to feel good about myself, and this gave me confidence to build a new life. (*positive attitude*)

This only summarizes the action involved in the personal problem and gives the structure. The writer elaborated this outline with emotional narration but held the length to the 1,000-word limit.

Good Housekeeping titles its feature "My Problem and How I Solved It." In the past, problems covered have included divorce, job transfer, giving a baby away for adoption, face-lifts—nearly the same subjects that have appeared in *Ladies' Home Journal*. It differs in the style of writing, projecting the action through scenes and dialogue; so you have a larger word allowance, but it follows the same basic pattern. Let's do a brief summary of the action.

Problem

My husband asked for a divorce and wanted all our possessions, including our son. I managed to keep our son and some possessions so as to build a new life.

Chronology

After a while my husband wanted to talk about getting together again, but I refused.

When he continued his efforts to harass me, I consulted a lawyer, who suggested a restraining order.

For the next two years, the harassment continued. He shoved me so hard I fell and broke my wrist.

When I dated another man, he slashed the tires on my car.

He called and told my boss I resigned my job.

Crisis

When I came home late one night, he attacked me and broke my cheekbone. I realized I would have no freedom until I moved away from him.

Conclusion

I moved and have started a new life for my son and me.

Good Housekeeping has another shorter problem-feature called "It Happened to Me." It follows the same pattern and style of writing.

Redbook wants reader contributions for "A Young Mother's Story." The editor points out: "We are interested in stories offering

147

practical and useful information on how you as a mother are solving the problems of marriage and family life or how you as a citizen or consumer handled a problem in your community." This feature runs between 1,000 and 2,000 words. The experience must have happened to a young mother and involve problems she faces. Let's summarize the pattern of a recent one.

Problem

I didn't want to let my young daughter cut her hair and suggested she think it over.

Chronology

Her sister tried to change the child's mind.
She determined to cut her hair.

Crisis

We liked her hair, but I see this as a parent learning to let go.

Conclusion

I want to learn to accept and respect the decisions of my children even though they do not agree with my own opinions.

American Baby in "My Own Experience" invites young parents to share how they solved problems. The editor states: "We invite all our readers to submit a story which involves some aspect of pregnancy or parenthood that taught a lesson helpful to other parents." An analysis shows the same basic pattern works for this contribution.

Problem

I learned my husband could not father a child so we decided to adopt one.

Chronology

After that adoption we tried to secure another but failed.
The doctor talked to us about artificial insemination by a donor, so we agreed.
We found a donor, and I became pregnant.

Crisis

The baby arrived, and we both think of Steve as the father.

Conclusion

We recommend this to others. We feel doubly blessed as adoptive and natural parents.

McCall's wants material for "Women on the Job." As the title implies, the subject discusses problems of working women. "We are interested in stories that reflect the special problems, conflicts, and opportunities that confront women who have jobs outside their homes, how they are handling these pressures, and any rewards they experience," the editor advises.

Special problems might include resistance from the family, worry about children, strain on the marriage, relations with the employer or co-workers, women in a masculine profession, a new job. This summary deals with the problem of a promotion.

Problem

I received an offer to change from secretary to public information officer. I decided to take it.

Chronology

I thought work and determination would help me succeed.

My husband suffered a heart attack, so I had to rearrange things at home because he came first.

Fellow workers found difficulty in adjusting to me as their supervisor.

Since men held most public information jobs, they made acceptance of a woman difficult at the various meetings.

Some customers wanted to talk with a man about complaints.

Crisis

I soon learned that knowledge, fairness, and a sympathetic ear won people over.

Conclusion

I recommend that anyone should take the chance to move up in his or her profession.

Sunshine Magazine takes a slightly different experience from a man or woman for "My Most Extraordinary Experience." In this dramatic experience the situation creates the problem, as seen in this summary of "Electrocuted," by Marian Slenker.

Problem

That morning I was mixing a chocolate cake. My kitchen was small, with very little counter space, so I had placed the electric mixer on top of my 1930-vintage electric range and plugged it into a socket on the front of the range.

After the cake was mixed, I pulled out one of the beaters and with my hand on the mixer, I placed the beater in an aluminum dishpan full of water in the sink.

Immediately, as soon as the beater touched the water, a powerful force held me fast!

Chronology

One hundred and twenty volts of electricity went through my body. I could not move or cry out.

I tried to pull the beater out of the water, but failed.

I knew this was the end, so I prayed silently and blacked out.

Crisis

I came to with my family all round me and a mess in the kitchen. The mixer, in falling, knocked the plug out of the socket. Surely God had guided it.

Conclusion

Never in my life have I been so happy to be able to see such a mess on my kitchen floor. The bits of shattered glass were covered with batter and it was a tedious job to clean up. But as I worked, I accepted even the cuts on my fingers with thankfulness. I was glad to be alive to clean it up.

I have never forgotten the day that God broke the circuit.

This experience differs from the ones previously summarized in that the situation produced the problem, it took place in one time span, and the opening did not start with the writer in a negative light, although the ending did show a change. I wrote all summaries in first-person because all the features use this viewpoint. This quoted opening and the conclusion, however, do resemble the style of writing in the others.

In writing your problem experience, briefly state the difficulty. Now list the chronology and decide on the crisis before you write the conclusion with the theme and your change in character. In short, write a summary exactly as I have done. Keep the elaborations under each part of equal length. Before you write the final draft read at least six examples from the magazine of your choice.

NOSTALGIA

The nostalgic piece looks to the past of at least twenty years ago and tries to make it come alive for the reader. The subject discusses an event, a person, or a combination of related things.

1. Pattern The opening paragraph introduces the emphasis, the body develops the subject with statements, and the conclusion provides the message for the reader. Regardless of the focus, you follow the same pattern.

When you highlight an event, start with action in the present that reminds you of the past, then relate the happenings. If you do a profile of someone from the past, introduce the person's dominant trait and relate the basic statements to this. The first paragraph should explain the grouping—Grandma's beauty aids or old-time remedies for illness—and then touch on one at a time.

The conclusion must present a message that results from reviewing the past. Keep the message earthy, and touch the reader where he lives.

2. Market *Down East* wants "nostalgic Maine recollections, humorous or otherwise." Let's summarize "I Remember . . . Grandmother's Old Reliable" by E. Glendenning Wood.

Opening

I think often about my grandmother's Down East kitchen and that companionable hulk, her old black range. It puffed out heat beyond compare while red coals glowed through the grate. A coal scuttle nearby was on duty year round.

That reliable stove had an accommodating character: it baked, brewed, stewed, simmered, and sauteed with equal competence. Fed kindling and coal, there was almost no limit to its talents. Grandmother and her faithful range made a harmonious duet, perfectly attuned to each other, after a fashion. I think of them always in tandem. . . .

Development

For my most vivid image of my grandmother was her expert supervision of her kitchen partner.

Baking was her major undertaking, and the outcome of any recipe hinged entirely upon the oven's performance.

Though she regarded cooking as a fine art, she measured with an incredibly careless eye: a handful, a hunk, a dollop, a pinch, did the trick.

She took enormous pride in her baking.

Frequently, great kitchen debates ensued between her and her visiting sisters.

The top of the old range served no less well. . . .

Grandmother's range served well in other ways.

Conclusion

My grandmother's wits were honed by the challenge of the old kitchen range, the true hearthstone of the house. Hectored, coaxed, complained of, applauded, it responded to her ministrations with a competence that matched her own. If I remember them today with nostalgic fondness, it's because, as a team, their like will rarely, if ever again, imbue a home with such a diversity of richness.

The opening and the conclusion indicate the typical style of writing used to expand each of the statements in the development.

Sunshine Magazine also wants nostalgic features for "Let's Reminisce" with a subtitle of "Tales of Days Gone By." This contribution discusses "Grandma" and offers a contrast in presentation.

Opening

Grandma wore character like a wholly woven spider's web extending in a soft-dew summer morning. She was her own witness.

Development

Lemon meringue pies and biscuits were her baking specialties.
Grandma never raised her voice or lost her patience.

Much of Grandma's time was spent in a small room in one corner of the second story of her house.

Grandma was a gentle lady who never raised a stir.

Conclusion

Grandma is gone now, and I don't suppose I can ever do justice to her living. But I doubt whether I'll ever forget my impression of a spider's beautiful web "sitting on top of the morning."—GARY SEVERSON

PERSONAL-OPINION FEATURE

Most personal-opinion pieces follow a basic pattern but differ in the statement of the protest, an essential element. The length varies with the market.

1. Pattern The personal-opinion feature follows three patterns. One states the protest, gives arguments to support it in the body of the feature, and sums up in the conclusion. Use this form when you discuss a controversial issue. In another pattern, the writer bases the protest on personal experience and starts in the negative attitude which changes to the positive in the conclusion. In a third pattern, the writer may have already changed, and the feature points out the reason.

2. Market *Glamour* wants opinion articles for "Viewpoint." The editor's note reads: "Do you have a cause you'd like to support? Or a grievance you'd like to air? We are asking for reader contributions to this column." This example by Carol Croland deals with jury duty.°

Protest

I tried to get out of jury duty. The summons from my county courthouse was just a bothersome inconvenience—I didn't *want* to spend two entire weeks away from my friends and my job. "How did they get my name?" "Why me?" I asked myself. Little did I know that my name immediately went into a computer list for prospective jurors when I registered to vote.

The protest continues in the next paragraph and tells how she tried to get out of jury duty and failed.

Argument

Setting foot into that assembly room was entering another world for me—far away from my usual daily interactions.

Jury duty became unexpectedly an opportunity for me to examine the way I lived.

My notions of the courtroom were based solely on television.

During my two weeks of duty, I served on three criminal cases and was the jury's foreperson for two of them.

It was a relief to find that no one of us took a juror's responsibility lightly.

Conclusion

Jury duty has been one of the more sobering experiences of my life. It was a rare opportunity to grapple personally with the significant concept of justice and to come face to face with real human drama. Jury duty demanded my very best—it was an unexpected and educational challenge.

This shows you the basic way to organize your article for this market, but do not attempt to write for it without reading at least six features in *Glamour*.

Readers may send their opinions on any subject worthy of protest to "Speakeasy" in *Cosmopolitan*. This market uses the protest without the character change. The newspaper world has a companion to these speaking-out features called the "op-ed page," meaning opposite the editorial page. Some newspapers regularly print these features, while others do so only occasionally. Check your newspapers regularly for these features, or better still, write and ask the editor.

Grit has a similar feature, called "As I See It." J. O. Gillon wrote this one on "Union Not Serving Members' Interest."

Protest

Many jobs are being lost because of union contracts that grant large wage increases.

Arguments

What has happened to the unions that once came to the rescue of the American workers?

The union officials seem more interested in gaining new members than in protecting those they already have.

On the job, grievances aren't always handled fairly.

It's time the unions became more reasonable, before they destroy even more jobs.

Big wage increases don't mean a thing if the contract forces the company out of business.

Conclusion

The unions should remember that a company cannot continue to pay more and more wages for less and less work.

To write an op-ed piece you must carefully research your facts and supply proof to the editor. Although difficult to write, it does offer one way to speak your opinion and get paid for it.

The Lookout, a religious publication, needs guest editorials, printed under the title of "Outlook." Each one points out some reform that the church should work for, such as preventing child abuse, giving full credit to those who serve the church in any capacity, cleaning up television programming. The editor describes the feature as "a page of reflection, opinion, or commentary by the editor or someone he chooses." Hold the length to 500 or 600 words.

Reader-contribution features offer you the advantage of reaching the editor quickly. While professional writers do submit to these markets, you get equal consideration.

*12
Parting Advice

So you have written and revised your filler or feature and given it your very best. Now you want to test it with an editor. How you submit it creates your first sales impression on the editor.

INTO THE MAIL

Present your filler or short feature in the best professional form. Think of your editor as a good friend you want to impress, and make the presentation as favorable as possible.

1. **Form** Always double-space your manuscript, even if only an epigram, and type it on a full sheet of paper. An editor finds a card or half-sheet difficult to handle or file. Quite often the editor will file your fillers or short features to use at a later date. The editor will notify you when this happens. Stop and think! Have you ever tried to retrieve a half-sheet or a small file card in an overcrowded file cabinet? Then you can understand the editor's preference for a whole sheet; so make your contribution easy to find in the file cabinet.

Keep the type of your typewriter clean. You can buy cleaner for a nominal sum; scrub with an old toothbrush to remove clogged carbon. Then blot the keys with a soft cloth or sturdy paper towel to remove any excess fluid. Don't use tissues, as they leave lint. Nothing annoys an editor so much as an *a* or *o* filled with carbon. You can commit an even worse offense if you type with a ribbon you should have replaced months ago. Always keep a dark ribbon on your typewriter. If you allow yourself one extravagance, make it a ribbon that produces easy-to-read type.

Never, and I repeat, *never*, type your fillers or short features on onion skin or see-through, thin paper. Have you ever tried reading this, or worse still, filing it? To read it, you must place another sheet beneath it. Thin paper refuses to slip smoothly into a crowded file. Try it! A good grade of rag-content, sixteen-pound bond—not colored—works best. The twenty-pound bond costs more and works no better than the sixteen-pound for erasing. Erasable bond also costs more and smears badly in transport. Editors find this paper difficult to write printing instructions on.

Always keep a carbon or machine copy of everything you submit no matter how short. Some writers type a draft and then copy it. For an epigram or riddle, this costs too much. You may want to copy a long reader-contribution feature, however, as making corrections on the carbon requires too much time and work.

The form of the submittal depends on whether you send a one-page filler or several pages. In typing the filler or feature, you put your name and address in the upper left-hand corner. Come down six spaces and three inches from the right-hand margin and put the approximate number of words.

Name
Address

Approximately
300 words

You can easily check the word length of a filler or short feature. Measure three inches of the printed or typed copy and determine the average number of words per inch. Multiply the average words-per-inch figure by the total number of inches in the piece. This will give you the approximate number.

Begin your copy about one third of the way from the top of the page. Usually, a staff writer puts the title on the tip and shortcut, newsbreak, anecdote, or joke. You will put a title on poems, mini-articles and experiences, and occasionally on the longer reader-contribution pieces. The title of a poem may carry some of the humor. If a title also helps you in writing the filler, then use it; but you need not send it. Whenever the filler or feature appears under a permanent title, as "Life in These United States" or "My Problem and How I Solve It," use that one on your copy. Don't get upset if the editor should change any particular title.

After you've put in the title, come down three spaces and indent ten for the first paragraph. Number the first page in the center, one inch from the bottom, if you need more than one page. Use no number with only one page.

For the other pages, put your name and a key word from the title in the upper left-hand corner. Come down six spaces and three inches from the right edge of the paper for the number. Skip three spaces and begin your copy. On the last page, against the left-hand margin, repeat your name and address.

When you submit remarks of another person, quote a published item, or send a newsbreak, give the source at the end of the copy. *Do* date your manuscript, because someone else may submit the same item. Remember, the editor pays for the one with the earliest date.

Writers disagree as to whether to send more than one filler at a time. It saves postage, some point out. But don't overlook the fact that you compete with yourself. The editor instinctively selects the best. If you submit one at a time, you might sell all of them. Always submit to one editor at a time.

2. Mailing If your filler or feature runs under three pages, send it in a legal-size envelope or a 6½-by-9½-inch manila one. Always include a stamped, self-addressed envelope with your manuscript. In the upper left-hand corner of the envelope, place the name and address of the magazine. If you fail to do this, someone may overlook adding the name of the magazine. Then you must check your records.

A number of magazines advertise that they will not return short fillers. Some will return them if you enclose return postage. If you do not hear from the magazine for three months, consider the submittal rejected. Type a new copy of the filler and send to another market.

If your manuscript requires more than three pages, send it flat. You can buy two sizes of manila envelopes that fit one into the other for a return trip—if necessary. Unless you do include the stamped envelope, magazines state, they will not return mini-articles or features. The flat envelope will also save on retyping.

Send your fillers and short features by first-class mail. Even with postal rates accelerating, you will probably never pay more than the cost of one ounce. To send manuscript-rate delays the time span for submitting again. You could have submitted to two other markets in the length of time manuscript-rate takes.

How many fillers should you keep in the mail? As many as possible. The more you have in the mail, the more opportunity you have to sell. For each filler, list ten markets and send it to all of them—one at a time—before you make any revisions.

The question always arises as to whether or not to return a rejected filler after a year has passed. A joke, anecdote, epigram, or short feature may deal with material ahead of its time. Never throw anything away! Something on the national scene may make it timely, or you may have found a way to revise it.

If you follow these simple rules for preparing and mailing your fillers and short pieces, the editor will reward you for your consideration.

BACK AT THE FILE BOX

So you intend to make money at selling fillers and mini-articles. When you send one in the mail, have the next one ready to develop. If you find nothing in your file box that interests you, then do some research.

1. **Research** You will do three different types of research. First you will go to all sources where you found ideas and explore them further. Especially, search your own experiences. You must daily add

new ideas to the file box, and this means keeping your notebook in action.

Searching for new markets can stimulate new ideas. Spend an hour or so at the library checking magazines there. Ask your friends to lend you magazines they get by subscription. By tapping all of these sources, you can easily set up a good market file. Consistently add new markets to the ones you know. Some unsold material may meet the requirements of these new markets.

Go through your notebook and your file box and look for undeveloped ideas or spin-offs from others. A little study can lead you into all sorts of discoveries.

2. Filing Sometimes you will leave an idea in your notebook until you feel ready to work on it. Learn to type up the ideas weekly and file them under the type of possible filler or feature they might develop into. By letting the material stay too long in your notebook, you often lose the spark of it.

Most frequently, you only write memory joggers in your notebook. When you transfer the idea to a file, *do* elaborate and put down everything you can remember about it. If you come across something in a magazine or newspaper that relates to the idea, add this to the file. Look at the ideas from every angle.

3. Writing You seldom develop a filler or a short feature in a day, so you will want to work on several at a time. Place the items under construction in separate manila folders. Work on one until you get tense or tired, then take a break, but go back to work on another. By shifting course, you may find the way to knock over a stumbling block on the first one.

When you feel that you have done all you can on the filler or short feature, put it aside for a week to cool. Then take an objective and critical look, which will help you sharpen the projection. If it needs no revision, sent it to the editor, but get right to work on others.

4. Recycling Do not toss fillers and short articles that you sell into a waste basket; put them in a dead file. Periodically, go through it and see if you can update them, or give any a new slant or ending. Recycling can really pay, if you concentrate. When you wrote the fillers, you might have listed several ways to end them. Always save these versions and attach them to the one sold. These can suggest ways that you can recyle the filler.

While you collect new ideas, you may find something that relates to an old one you have already sold. Make a note of this and add it to the card in your dead file. Any information you can add to those already sold will simplify the revision. You always recycle when a filler or short feature has failed to catch the attention of any editor.

RETURN TRIP

A returned filler or short feature can spoil your day if you let it. But please, don't worry more than one day—two at the most—and get it back in the mail. When no one buys, recycle it or put it aside for further analysis.

1. Instant Interest Perhaps you failed to get into the action fast enough and lost the reader's interest. Try giving the piece more punch at the beginning. Perhaps the scope of the piece appealed to too few readers. Broaden the reader identification, even add a new element for a wider appeal. If you define or describe your reader, this will help you check the scope.

2. Brevity When you first begin to write, you use too many adjectives and fail to rely on action verbs. Go through the manuscript and cut out all the unnecessary words. Look at it critically with the eye of a editor. Do you stop at the right place? You can beat a filler or short feature to death by dragging out the ending. Give the reader credit for some intelligence, and don't spell out the most minute detail or repeat too much. Encourage the reader to collaborate with a little imagination, and add some implied ingredients. See if you followed the correct pattern or can tighten the organization.

3. Message Too often you think that you said one thing, and it comes out another way. Do you lead up to the ending in the best way? Your punch line may have fallen flat because you failed to plant the right detail in the beginning. Does the message touch the life of a number of readers? Try to inject emotion into the message, and above all, sharpen it so that no one can miss the point.

4. Market Many times you try to sell a market without actually studying the requirements. You may have violated a taboo. Don't send an anecdote about divorce to a Catholic market or an obviously improvised experience to a confession magazine. Though it may seem unbelievable, some writers stupidly do this.

Unknowingly you may make fun of an ethnic group or physical handicap. One editor returned a short feature with a letter stating that a physically handicapped person may have difficult obstacles to overcome in order to improve a situation. The magazine's short pieces pointed out how to improve personality traits that anyone can mend.

When you first begin to market fillers and short features, you fail to notice that groups of magazines carry the same type of fillers. The national weeklies and the confession magazines, for example, use the same basic types of personal experiences. Science and mechanical markets buy similar tips and shortcuts. In developing a market list, you want to associate these markets.

Make a file of editorial notes from any magazine that uses them, and then read the magazine. Take the types of fillers and group the magazines according to what they buy. For each individual market list how each differs and how requirements agree. With this information you can make the slight revision immediately and send the piece on to the next market. Know your market requirements.

For the mini-articles and reader contributions, read a number before you begin to write. This puts you in the mood, and subconsciously you will write in a similar style. Do not read anything else between getting in the mood and the actual writing, or this will disrupt your subconscious.

THE OCCUPATIONAL HAZARD

At this point you say, "But I only wanted to write one little filler." You never stop with one little filler or short feature. If you receive a rejection, determination or persistence pushes you to send it out again. The minute an editor sends you a check, the writing bug bites you. Already, you begin to think of other fillers and mini-articles you might sell.

First or later sales never come easy, but I know of no other profession that pays so well for such pleasurable activity. To sell regularly, you must work some every day and build up your production. You'll get discouraged and promise to quit after the next rejection slip, only to begin work again tomorrow. The desire to write never lets go of you.

Then the day arrives when you receive three checks in the mail. You throw yourself into the business with renewed zeal. You may still overwrite or underpunch a few, but you get more checks than rejection slips. The editor knows your name and asks you to try a few short features on assignment. Every day more checks arrive. Later on you plan to try some real writing, but right now you can't afford to take the time!

Markets

The list of markets for fillers and short features resulted from questionnaires sent to editors. They listed the type of short pieces they buy, the pay, the title, and the length, and they generously supplied tear sheets.

The market for fillers and short features changes constantly. Although this represents a current list at the time of publication of the book, it can change quickly. New magazines come on the market. Magazines stop buying fillers and features while others begin to purchase them. Many of the markets have not changed their filler requirements for a number of years, but always check several recent issues of the magazine before you submit your filler.

AG-PILOT INTERNATIONAL. P.O. Box 25, Milton-Freewater, OR 97862. Column material and newsbreaks for "Dump Handle" $25 or 3¢–4¢ per word.

AMERICAN BABY MAGAZINE. 575 Lexington Ave., New York, NY 10022. Anecdotes, column material, mini-personal experiences, mini-profiles. "Chuckles from Cherubs," "My Own Experience" 10¢ a word.

AMERICAN DANE. Box 31748, Omaha, NB 68131. Need Danish slant. Puzzles $15, clippings, jokes, gags, anecdotes.

THE AMERICAN LEGION MAGAZINE. P.O. Box 1055, Indianapolis, IN 46206. "Parting Shots" verse $4.50 per line, anecdotes $10–$12.50, jokes and epigrams $10–$25, daffy definitions, quips.

THE AMERICAN RIFLEMAN. 1600 Rhode Island Ave. N.W., Washington, DC 20036. "In My Experience" buys mini-informative articles on firearms and related subjects.

APPLEWOOD JOURNAL. P.O. Box 1781, San Francisco, CA 94101. Arts and crafts, clippings, anecdotes, column material, daffy definitions, puzzles, jokes, tips and shortcuts, oddities, mini-articles, recipes, newsbreaks, signs $5–$20.

ARMY MAGAZINE. 2425 Wilson Blvd., Arlington, VA 22201. Anecdotes $5–$25.

ARMY RESERVE. The Pentagon, Washington, DC 20310. Mini-profiles, newsbreaks, tips, and shortcuts.

BABY CARE. 52 Vanderbilt Ave., New York, NY 10017. "Family Corner" anecdotes $10, "Focus on You."

BABY TALK. 66 East 34th St., New York, NY 10016. Mini-articles $20, "Many Other Mother Suggestions" $5.

BETTER HOMES AND GARDENS. 1716 Locust St., Des Moines, IA 50336. "Tips Tools Techniques" $25.

BEYOND REALITY MAGAZINE. 203 West 42nd St., New York, NY 10036. Clippings, gags, newsbreaks, mini-personal experiences, oddities, and strange phenomena. Up to $20.

BOOK DIGEST. 730 Fifth Ave., New York, NY 10019. "Wit & Wisdom" $50.

BOSTON MAGAZINE. 1050 Park Square Blvd., Boston, MA 02116. Mini-profiles, newsbreaks, oddities $15–$25.

BOWHUNTER MAGAZINE. 3808 South Calhoun St., N. Ft. Wayne, IN 46807. Anecdotes, newsbreaks, oddities, tips, and shortcuts under "Would You Believe" up to $25.

BP SINGER FEATURES. 3164 Tyler Ave., Anaheim, CA 93801. Crafts, column material, puzzles, recipes, newsbreaks, tips, and shortcuts.

CAPPER'S WEEKLY. 616 Jefferson St., Topeka, KS 66607. Anecdotes, light verse, mini-personal experiences, recipes, tips and shortcuts for "Heart of the Home" and "Hometown Heartbeat."

CAREER WORLD. 501 Lake Forest Ave., Highwood, IL 60040. Jokes for "Joke Works" $2.

CAR EXCHANGE. Iola, WI 54945. Puzzles, jokes, light verse, tips and shortcuts, recipes, oddities for "The Last Page" 4¢ per word.

CASH NEWSLETTER. Box 1999, Brooksville, FL 33512. Clippings, newsbreaks, tips, and shortcuts, 50¢–$2.

CATHOLIC DIGEST. P.O. Box 43090, St. Paul, MN 55164. Mini-experiences of 300 words: "Hearts Are Trumps," "The Perfect Assist," "People Are Like That," "Open Door," "In Our Parish," "Signs of the Times," jokes $40–$50.

CHANGING TIMES. 1729 H St., N.W., Washington, DC 20006. Epigrams and quips for "Notes on These Changing Times" $10.

CHILD LIFE. 1100 Waterway Blvd., Box 567B, Indianapolis, IN 46206. Arts and crafts ideas, puzzles, games, mazes, recipes. "All About" section on health, safety, nutrition, and recipes $5–$35.

CHRISTIAN ADVENTURER. Box 850, Joplin, MO 64801. Biblical puzzles, anecdotes, light verse, mini-experience, and profile ½¢ per word.

THE CHURCH MUSICIAN. 127 Ninth Ave. North, Nashville, TN 27202. Anecdotes, puzzles, mini-experiences that relate to music $7.50–$20.

CORVETTE FEVER. Box 6317, Toledo, OH 43614. Anecdotes, column material, games, puzzles, mini-personal experience, signs, and vanity plates, all as relate to Corvettes 10¢ a word.

COSMOPOLITAN. 224 West 57th St., New York, NY 10019. "Speakeasy," protest mini-article.

COUNTRYSTYLE. 11058 West Addison, Franklin Park, IL 60131. Anecdotes on country-music stars, column material, newsbreaks, recipes, 5¢ a word.

CREATIVE COMPUTING. P.O. Box 789–M, Morristown, NY 07960. Anecdotes, column material, daffy definitions, gags, light verse, newsbreaks, oddities for "Compendium" and puzzles for "Puzzles and Problems" $3 and up.

CREDIT NEWSLETTER. 5775 Mosholu Ave., Riverdale, NY 10471. Clippings, jokes, gags, anecdotes, newsbreaks, short humor $5.

CRICKET. Box 100, LaSalle, IL 61301. Anecdotes, arts and crafts, column material, daffy definitions, games, puzzles, riddles, jokes, light verse, mini-profiles, and recipes 25¢ per word, $3 per line for poetry. "Old Cricket Says" editorial.

DECISION. 1300 Harmon Place, Minneapolis, MN 55403. Poetry for "Quiet Heart," and excerpts from published books with Christian theme for "Reflections."

DISCOVERY. Dept. of Christian Education, 999 College Ave., Winona Lake, IN 46590. Arts and crafts articles, games, puzzles, light verse, mini-personal experiences, and recipes 2¢ per word.

DISCOVERY, the Allstate Motor Club magazine. Allstate Plaza, Northbrook, IL 60062. Anecdotes for "Right Side of the Road" $10.

DIXIE ROTO. *The Times Picayune,* New Orleans, LA 70140. Amusing anecdotes about children for "Bright Talk" $2.

DOLL WORLD OMNIBOOK. Box 1953, Brooksville, Fl 33512. Verse, how-to-do-it articles $5 minimum.

DOWN EAST. Camden, ME 04843. Mini-personal experiences for "I Remember . . ." and anecdotes for "It Happened Down East" $10, $50 for nostalgia.

DYNAMIC YEARS. 215 Long Beach Blvd., Long Beach, CA 90802. Newsbreaks for "News Worth Filing," and mini-profiles for "Dynamic Americans."

EBONY. 820 South Michigan Ave., Chicago, IL 60605. Mini-profiles with pix for "Speaking of People" $35.

EBONY JR! 820 South Michigan Ave., Chicago, IL 60605. Arts and crafts $250; jokes $5; riddles $10; $25–$35 for mini-profiles, games, and puzzles; $75 for recipes. Special title "Daze-A-Head" for game page.

EDITOR & PUBLISHER. 575 Lexington Ave., New York, NY 10022. Typographical errors $2.

EXPECTING. 52 Vanderbilt Ave., New York, NY 10017. Anecdotes about pregnancy for "Happenings" $10.

FAMILY CIRCLE. 488 Madison Ave., New York, NY 10022. Tips for "Readers Idea Exchange" $25, recipes.

FAMILY HANDYMAN. 1999 Shepard Road, St. Paul, MN 55116. "Handy Hints," for projects around the home $10–$100.

FAMILY PET. P.O. Box 22964, Tampa, FL 33622. Anecdotes, light verse, and tips for "Pet Tips" $2–$5.

FAMILY WEEKLY. 641 Lexington Ave., New York, NY 10033. Children's anecdotes, daffy definitions, jokes, short verse for "Quips & Quotes" $10.

FARM JOURNAL. Washington Square, Philadelphia, PA 19105. "Homemade and Handy Ideas" with pix $75. Farm people with interesting hobbies.

FATE. 500 Hyacinth Place, Highland Park, IL 60035. "Quirks of Fate," oddities, strange phenomena in newsbreaks, $2.50–$10.

FIELD AND STREAM. 1515 Broadway, New York, NY 10036. Tips and shortcuts for "How It's Done" $250.

FRETS MAGAZINE. Box 615, Saratoga, CA 95070. $100 for guest column on music.

GAMBLING TIMES. 839 North Highland Ave., Hollywood, CA 90038. Jokes, gags, anecdotes, short humor about gambling, $5–$25.

GLAMOUR. 350 Madison Ave., New York, NY 10017. Mini-protest for "Viewpoint" $200.

GOLF. 380 Madison Ave., New York, NY 10017. Anecdotes, epigrams, light verse for "Only in Golf $25–$50; pix feature of "Professional Hairstyles," for Flip Shots; "Best Golf Tips I Ever Had" from celebrity golfer $50–$75.

GOLF DIGEST. 495 Westport Ave., Norwalk, CT 06856. Anecdotes, light verse, oddities for "Rub of the Grin" $20–$50.

GOOD HOUSEKEEPING. 959 8th Ave., New York, NY 10019. "Out of the Mouths of Babes," "Signs of the Times," "Marriage Counsel," "Notable Names," "Points to Ponder." Verse, jokes, definitions for "Light Housekeeping," short articles for "The Better Way," reader contributions for "It Happened to Me" and "My Problem and How I Solved It."

GOOD NEWS. 308 East Main St., Wilmore, KY 40390. Anecdotes, clippings about United Methodist activities, daffy definitions, quizzes, light verse, mini-personal experiences and profiles, short humor for "Quipping the Saints" $2–$10.

GOSPEL CARRIER. Box 850, Joplin, MO 64801. Light verse, mini-personal experiences and profiles, self-help ½¢ per word.

GRIT. 208 West 3rd St., Williamsport, PA 17701. Jokes, epigrams, quips, light verse for "Talelights." "Pet Peeve" $5, "Thrift Tip" $5. "Poetry Just for You, riddles and quizzes for "Let's Have Some Fun," anecdotes and jokes for "Grins and Chuckles." Mini-articles for "Kindest Act" $25, "Turning Point," $25, "Narrow Escape" $25, "My Funniest Moment" $20, "As I See It" (protest) $35.

GUIDEPOSTS. 747 Third Ave., New York, NY 10017. Mini-experience for "Fragile Moments," mini-profile for "Quiet People," tips for "Why Don't We," "Guide Poster," good shorts of two to three paragraphs.

HOME LIFE. 127 9th Ave. North, Nashville, TN 37235. Light verse at $10, 3½¢ per word for mini-personal experience.

HUMORAMA, INC. 100 North Village Ave., Rockville Centre, NY 11570. Epigrams, gags, jokes, limericks, short verse 8¢ per word.

HUNTING DOG MAGAZINE. 9714 Montgomery Rd., Cincinnati, OH 45242. Newsbreaks, tips and shortcuts, mini-articles for "Pro's Tips" 3¢ to $10 minimum.

INCOME OPPORTUNITIES. 380 Lexington Ave., New York, NY 10017. Mini-profiles and oddities.

INSTRUCTOR MAGAZINE. 757 3rd Ave., New York, NY 10017. Newsbreaks in education for "Edubits."

INTIMATE STORY, INTIMATE SECRETS, TRUE SECRETS. 2 Park Ave., New York, NY 10016. Light verse $10.

KNOWLEDGE NEWS FEATURES. P.O. Box 1, Kenilworth, IL 60043. Arts and crafts, column material, daffy definitions, epigrams, figures of speech, gags, puzzles, jokes, light verse, oddities, errors in the press, recipes, signs.

LADIES' HOME JOURNAL. 641 Lexington Ave., New York, NY 10022. Reader contribution "It's Not Easy to Be a Woman."

LADY'S CIRCLE. 23 West 26th St., New York, NY 10010. Protests for "Sound-off" $10; recipes for "Reader's Exchange Cookbook" $5.

LADYCOM. 1800 M. St. NW, Suite 650 South, Washington, DC 20036. Anecdotes, tips and shortcuts, mini-nostalgia related to military life $25–$50.

LEARNING. 530 University Av., Palo Alto, CA 94301. Mini-articles related to teaching elementary school students.

LEFAN FEATURES. 1802 South 13, Temple, TX 76501. Mini-experience, tips and shortcuts for "Money Saver of the Week (and/or Month)" $2.

LET'S LIVE MAGAZINE. 44 North Larchmont Blvd., Los Angeles, CA 90004. Mini-personal experience $50–$75, recipes $5.

THE LOOKOUT. 8121 Hamilton Ave., Cincinnati, OH 45231. Mini-self-help articles and editorial protest for "Outlook," of a religious nature 3¢ per word.

LOST TREASURE. 15115 South 76th East Ave., Bixby, OK 74008. $5 for clippings in "Clippings Cache," and 3¢ per word for column material.

MAKE IT WITH LEATHER. Box 1386, Fort Worth, TX 76101. "Scrap Bin Projects" $25, "Tips and Hints" $10, "Tricks of the Trade, Crafty Critters" $10, mini-profiles of leather crafters.

MATURE LIVING. 127 9th Ave. North, Nashville, TN 37234. Children's anecdotes for "Grandparents' Brag Board" $5, poetry, sayings of well-known people, mini-self-help.

MATURE YEARS. 201 8th Ave. South, Nashville, TN 37202. Anecdotes, epigrams, puzzles, jokes, tips and shortcuts 3¢ per word.

McCALL'S. 230 Park Ave., New York, NY 10017. "Survival in the Suburbs" $50, mini-articles for "Right Now" up to $250, poetry $5 a line, reader contribution "Women on the Job: A Reader's Story."

MECHANIX ILLUSTRATED. 1515 Broadway, New York, NY 10036. Newsbreaks on new products.

MEDICAL ECONOMICS. 680 Kinderkamack Road, Oradell, NY 07649. Anecdotes from practicing physicians $75; other medical anecdotes $25–$50.

MEDICAL WORLD NEWS. 1221 Ave. of the Americas, New York, NY 10020. Epigrams and signs.

MIDNIGHT/GLOBE. 200 Railroad Ave., Greenwich, CT 06830. Jokes for "Funny Side" $5, mini-experience for "Your Story" $25, recipes, anecdotes, signs, quips, for "Dear Suzie" $5, for "Letters" $5.

MID-WEST OUTDOORS. 111 Shore Drive, Hinsdale, IL 60521. Tips and shortcuts, and recipes for fish or game.

MILITARY JOURNAL. 218 Beech St., Bennington, VT 05201. Clippings, mini-experience and profile, oddities 50¢ per column inch and $2 per illustration.

MODERN MATURITY. 215 Long Beach Blvd., Long Beach, CA 90701. Fillers for "Tips Worth Considering," newsbreaks for "Worthy of Note," puzzles for "Fun Fare," mini-profiles for "Spotlight on People," jokes for "Laughing Matter," poems for "Our Versifying Friends."

THE MOTHER EARTH NEWS. P.O. Box 70, Hendersonville, NC 28739. Tips, recipes for "Mother's Down-Home Country Lore," short craft articles.

MONTGOMERY WARD AUTO CLUB NEWS. 1400 West Greenleaf Ave., Chicago, IL 60226. Column material.

NATIONAL ENQUIRER. Lantana, FL 33464. TV bloopers, "Current Quote of Week," pix of signs, verse, mini-self-help.

NATIONAL RETIRED TEACHERS ASSOCIATION JOURNAL. 215 Long Beach Blvd., Long Beach, CA 90801. Newsbreaks for "Panorama," verse, puzzles, jokes for "Exit Laughing," and mini-profiles for "NRTA Notables."

NATIONAL SUPERMARKET SHOPPER. P.O. Box 1149, Great Neck, NY 11023. Mini-articles for "Supermarket Strategy," tips and light verse for "Kitchen Helpers," column material, jokes 5¢ a word, $5 minimum.

THE NEW ENGLAND GUIDE. Box 1108–2, Steam Mill Ct., Concord, NH 03301. Epigrams, quips, figures of speech, recipes, anecdotes $10, boxed oddities $25.

THE NEW YORK ANTIQUES ALMANAC. Box 335, Lawrence, NY 11559. Anecdotes for "Reader's Roundtable," arts and crafts, mini-personal experience, tips and shortcuts, $5–$25.

ORBEN'S CURRENT COMEDY and ORBEN'S COMEDY FILLERS. 1200 North Nash St., Arlington, VA 22209. Epigrams, daffy definitions, jokes, verse, and quips.

OUTDOOR LIFE. 380 Madison Ave., New York, NY 10017. Personal experience for "This Happened to Me," and recipes for outdoors $25.

PARENTS' MAGAZINE. 52 Vanderbilt Ave., New York, NY 10017. "Parents' Exchange" $20.

PARISH FAMILY DIGEST. 200 Noll Plaza, Huntington, IN 46750. Anecdotes, figures of speech, jokes, newsbreaks, $5. Mini-experiences and profiles for "True Experience" and "Our Parish," devotions for "Mini-Meditations from My Daily Visitor."

PEOPLE ON PARADE. 1720 Washington Blvd., Box 2315, Ogden, UT 84404. Anecdotes, epigrams, quips, jokes, mini-experience, profiles, oddities, tips and shortcuts, humor articles for "Wit Stop" 10¢ per word.

PHOTO INSIGHT. Suite 2, 16915 Jamaica Ave., Jamaica, NY 11432. Photo arts and crafts, column material, tips and shortcuts, $5.

PILLOW TALK. 260 Madison Ave., New York, NY 10017. Clippings, puzzles, newsbreaks, oddities for "Front Entry" $5.

PLAYBOY. 919 North Michigan, Chicago, IL 60611. "Party Jokes" $50, "After Hours" $50 to $350, "Potpourri" $75, "Pipeline."

POPULAR ELECTRONICS. 1 Park Ave., New York, NY 10016. Puzzles for "Electronic IQ Quiz" and "Tips & Techniques" $5–$90.

POPULAR MECHANICS. 224 West 57th St., New York, NY 10019. "Photo Hints" and "Hints from Readers" $40 with pix.

POPULAR SCIENCE. 380 Madison Ave., New York, NY 10017. "Taking Care of Your Car," "Wordless Workshop," "Shop Talk" $25 and up.

PRIMARY TREASURE. 1350 Villa St., Mountain View, CA 94040. Crafts, puzzles, light verse, articles for "Nature Nuggets," and "Pen Pals" 1¢ per word.

PUBLICIST. 221 Park Ave. South, New York, NY 10003. Tips and shortcuts related to public relations.

QUILT WORLD. Box 1953, Brooksville, FL 33512. Anecdotes, crafts, verse, oddities, tips and shortcuts, $5 and up.

R A D A R. 8121 Hamilton Ave., Cincinnati, OH 45231. Games, puzzles, jokes, crafts, mini-experiences 1½¢ per word.

READER'S DIGEST. Pleasantville, NY 10570. $35 for "Time Out for Sports," "Points to Ponder," "Quotable Quotes," "An Encouraging Word," "Notes from All Over," "Toward More Picturesque Speech," "Laughter, the Best Medicine," and "Personal Glimpses." $300 for "All in a Day's Work," "Humor in Uniform," "Life in These United States," "Campus Comedy." Fillers at bottom of page, such as signs, press errors $15 per *Digest* two-column line.

REDBOOK. 230 Park Ave., New York, NY 10017. "We Are Proud to Announce" $50.

REFLECTIONS, TRAILS. P.O. Box 788, Wheaton, IL 60189. Jokes, games, puzzles, epigrams, quips, daffy definitions for "Fun Stuff" $3–$15. Tips, shortcuts, crafts, mini-experience $15–$35.

ROLL CALL. 201 Massachusetts Ave. NE, Washington, DC 20002. Anecdotes, gags, oddities, light verse with political angle.

RUNNER'S WORLD. Box 366, Mountain View, CA 94040. Profiles and newsbreaks for "Looking at People" $25–$50, anecdotes for "Running Shorts" $10, tips, shortcuts, mini-experiences for "Reader's Forum" $25.

THE SATURDAY EVENING POST. 1100 Waterway Blvd., Indianapolis, IN 46204. Daffy definitions, puzzles, light verse, errors in the press, epigrams for "Post Scripts" $15–$25.

SATURDAY REVIEW. 1290 Ave. of the Americas, New York, NY 10019. Newsbreaks for "Front Runner."

SAVVY. 111 Eighth Ave., Suite 1517, New York, NY 10011. Revelations, moments of truth, and other professional eye-openers for "Facts of Life."

SEVENTEEN. 850 Third Ave., New York, NY 10022. Mini-mag, first page lead article, 750 words $125; how-to, 500 words $50; wrap up $10.

SKYDIVING. P.O. Box 189, Daytona, FL 32725. Newsbreaks.

SMALL WORLD. 818 Sylvan Ave., Englewood Cliffs, NJ 07632. Anecdotes and uses of Volkswagens for "Small Talk" $15.

SPORTS AFIELD. 250 West 55th St., New York, NY 10019. Anecdotes, crafts, clippings, newsbreaks, oddities, tips and shortcuts, mini-articles for "Almanac."

SPORTS MAGAZINE. 641 Lexington Ave., New York, NY 10022. "Photo Finish" pix.

THE STAR. 730 3rd Ave., New York, NY 10017. "What Kids Say," mini-self-help articles, newsbreaks, and "Letters" $25–$75.

SUNDAY DIGEST. 850 North Grove Ave., Elgin, IL 60120. Anecdotes, mini-profiles, and experiences with Christian emphasis $10–$35, light verse.

SUNSET MAGAZINE. Menlo Park, CA 94030. Recipes for "Chefs of the West" and "Sunset's Kitchen Cabinet" $25.

SUNSHINE PRESS. Litchfield, IL 62056. Mini-articles for "Let's Reminisce" and "My Most Extraordinary Experience."

TALK. 100 Park Ave., New York, NY 10022. Tips and shortcuts $50.

TEACHER. 77 Bedford St., Stamford, CT 06901. Teaching tips.

TODAY'S CHRISTIAN PARENT. 8121 Hamilton Ave., Cincinnati, OH 45231. Anecdotes and short experiences for "Happenings at Our House," daffy definitions, epigrams, quips for "Family Sense & Nonsense."

TOUCH. Box 7244, Grand Rapids, MI 49510. Puzzles, short humor, anecdotes, mini-experiences.

U.S. NAVAL INSTITUTE. Annapolis, MD 21402. Anecdotes $25.

UNITY MAGAZINE. Unity Village, MO 64065. Light verse, mini-experiences 2¢–5¢ per word.

THE VINE. 201 8th Ave. South, Nashville, TN 37202. Puzzles, arts and crafts at 4¢ per word, verse.

WALL STREET JOURNAL. 22 Courtland St., New York, NY 10007. Epigrams, quips, light verse for "Pepper & Salt."

WOMEN'S CIRCLE HOME COOKING. Box 1952, Brooksville, FL 33512. Recipes.

WOMAN'S DAY. 1515 Broadway, New York, NY 10036. "Neighbors" $25.

WOMEN'S SPORTS MAGAZINE. 314 Town & Country Village, Palo Alto, CA 94301. Anecdotes, clippings, mini-profiles, newsbreaks, errors in the press for "Sidelines" $25 and up.

WORKBENCH. 425 Pennsylvania Ave., Kansas City, MO 64111. "Crosscuts" includes "Shop Tips" and "Readers Service" that has craft ideas, tips, shortcuts, and home improvement in working with wood.

WORLD TRAVELING. 30943 Club House Lane, Farmington Hills, MI 48018. Puzzles, recipes, jokes 10¢ per word.

WRITER'S DIGEST. 9933 Alliance Road, Cincinnati, OH 45242. Mini-articles for "The Writing Life," clippings, anecdotes 10¢ per word; light verse $5–$50.

YANKEE MAGAZINE. Dublin, NH 03444. Newsbreaks about area that are put in cartoons.

YOUNG JUDAEAN. 817 Broadway, New York, NY 10003. Arts and crafts ideas, games, puzzles, riddles, jokes, oddities, recipes.

YOUNG MISS. 52 Vanderbilt Ave., New York, NY 10017. Arts and crafts, crossword puzzles $5–$25.

Index

ABOUT THE AUTHOR

Louise Boggess received her B.A. and M.A. degrees from the University of Texas where she graduated with high honors, and was elected to Phi Beta Kappa and Phi Lambda Theta. She began her writing career as woman's editor and feature writer on a newspaper, but after several years returned to teaching. For the past twenty-years she has taught professional writing at the College of San Mateo in the classroom and by national television, through correspondence courses for the University of California at Berkeley, and for Writer's Digest School. She has served on the staff of thirty-two writers' conferences as a lead panelist, seminar lecturer, critic and consultant. Her current books include *How to Write Short Stories That Sell, Writing Fiction That Sells, Article Techniques That Sell,* and *American Brilliant Cut Glass.*